HOPE for Harvest

for harvest

Authentic

Copyright © 2012 HOPE 08 Ltd

17 16 15 14 13 12   7 6 5 4 3 2 1

First published 2012 by Authentic Media Ltd
Presley Way, Crownhill, Milton Keynes, Bucks, MK8 OES.
www.authenticmedia.co.uk

The right of HOPE 08 Ltd to be identified as the Authors of this Work has been asserted by
them in accordance with the Copyright, Designs and Patents Act 1988.

British Library Cataloguing in Publication Data
A catalogue record for this book is available from the British Library
ISBN: 978-1-86024-849-8

Printed in Great Britain by Bell and Bain, Glasgow.

Contents

HRH Prince Charles, Prince of Wales

CLARENCE HOUSE

Too many people, in recent years, have thought that harvest has become an outdated festival that has little relevance. I have always thought that recognizing the importance of God's bounty through giving thanks for the harvest safely gathered in has a vital rôle in connecting people to the earth that brought forth these resources – and to the extraordinary miracle that Nature's services represent. Of course, many rural communities still gather to give thanks for the fruits of the land, and I am so pleased that HOPE is encouraging churches and communities across the United Kingdom to embrace the true meaning of harvest once more. The season of harvest is a wonderful time for us to reconnect with our countryside and to consider from where our food comes. It also gives us a chance to reflect and give thanks for the abundance that we have and it reminds us that even in difficult times we can still live with thankful and generous hearts for the Sustainer that ultimately sustains us.

Introduction

Dear friends

We're thrilled you're with us on this, the latest stage of the HOPE journey where we're looking to make the most of all the missional opportunities around harvest.

So why harvest?

The Hebrew word for festival means designated time, so festivals are time designated to God. They are intended to tell us when we can move forward with life and when we are to stop; to redirect our thoughts towards the eternal and to provide a focus to celebrate, thank and embrace God's annual calendar. Festivals played a part in every aspect of Jewish life. Colossians 2:16–17 talks about festivals and says these things are like a shadow of what is to come, but what is true and real has come and is found in Christ. By the time of Jesus' coming, the festivals had become so corrupted and twisted that they were stumbling blocks for the people. They had become barriers. But Jesus took what had been corrupted and made it new.

Harvest is a fantastic time to be thankful to God.

Harvest, as a season of thankfulness, is a holy invitation to re-evaluate and re-orientate our values. The festivals were always seen as times of spiritual renewal and we are invited to draw near and be re-shaped so that we can be a light to those around us. Harvest provides us with a great opportunity to make precisely that statement. I am excited about the potential of this resource for highlighting (both on a personal level and in our communities) the importance of giving thanks to God for our work and for the many gifts he has given to us, and its potential for equipping us to share his generosity with those who don't know him.

In many rural churches harvest is a well-celebrated season, but for those in towns and cities we've lost some of the emphasis on this as an opportunity to thank God for the ways he provides for us. Harvest is a fantastic time to be thankful to God for all the good things he brings to us through our work and to look at all the opportunities our workplaces bring us as our mission fields. This resource contains fresh ideas and inspiration for urban and rural churches to support their congregations in their places of work as well as providing some thoughts on the value of work itself. The material also reflects the fact this season prompts us to reflect on God's generosity, and to think about how we can be generous to others, as well as to consider how we can be good stewards of all the resources God has given us.

How to use this resource

There are so many ideas in these pages that there's something that every individual, small group, youth group or church can do! If you plan ahead it will give you plenty of time to make the most of the harvest season and to get the best out of your outreach. You may want to plan together with other churches and put on even bigger and better events together!

Why not encourage your small groups to use the Bible studies in September too? These will help them to think about some of the themes of harvest including sacrifice, justice, generosity and global community. There are also some great mission ideas and Bible sessions for your youth leader to use with your young people so that the whole church is involved in this season of mission. In addition to this material, we've also included some reflective articles in this resource about thankfulness and generosity, which we hope will inspire you in your personal relationship with God during this season.

HOPE for the Future

We're planning another full year of mission in 2014 which means we'll have a brand new resource ready for you early in 2013 so you can plan, pray, prepare and get involved. We're excited about the prospect of hundreds of churches across our nation joining together to bring the good news of Jesus to their communities in word and deed. We'll be looking at how we make the most of events in the church calendar such as Easter and Christmas, but also how we find the right projects that we can get involved in week in, week out throughout the year that will bless our communities.

We'd love to hear what's going on in your area, so please do visit our website (www.hopetogether.org.uk) or email us (info@hopetogether.org.uk) and let us know how things are going.

God bless you and your churches as you seek to reap a harvest for God in your community.

Roy Crowne

On behalf of the HOPE Board of Directors: Steve Clifford, Evangelical Alliance; Andy Hawthorne, The Message Trust; Mike Pilavachi, Soul Survivor; Steve Price, HOPE Together.

And the HOPE Leadership Team: Yemi Adedeji, Jesus House; Wendy Beech-Ward, Spring Harvest; Matt Bird, Make it Happen; Ian Bunce, Baptist Union of Great Britain; Gavin Calver, Youth for Christ; Rob Cotton, Bible Society; Joanne Cox, Methodist Church; Jane Holloway, World Prayer Centre; Ann Holt, OBE, Bible Society; Dr Rachel Jordan, Church of England; Bishop Wayne Malcolm, Christian Life City Church; Ade Omooba, Christian Concern/Christian Legal Centre; Kiera Phyo, Tearfund; Laurence Singlehurst, Cell UK; David Westlake, Tearfund.

> We're excited about the prospect of hundreds of churches across our nation joining together to bring the good news of Jesus to their communities.

Background to HOPE

HOPE came from a vision and conversation between Roy Crowne, Mike Pilavachi and Andy Hawthorne who were all passionate about churches in the UK reaching their communities with the good news of Jesus. HOPE initially focused on equipping and encouraging churches to take part in a year of mission in 2008 which saw churches re-envisioned to get involved in their community, and saw many come to faith as a result. With this momentum gained, it was clear HOPE should continue and find new ways to resource and encourage churches in the amazing work they were doing.

You can read more about the story of HOPE on our website www.hopetogether.org.uk.

Contact:
HOPE
8A Market Place
Rugby
Warwickshire
CV21 3DU
Tel: 01788 542782
Email: info@hopetogether.org.uk

Harvesting a Community of Transformed People Through Prayer and Fasting

Pastor Agu Irukwu

During the harvest season we see crops produced by the land resulting from a sowing and growing period. Likewise, the harvest of transformed communities of new believers also requires an intentional period of sowing through prayer and fasting. Someone once said to me, 'Didn't fasting and prayer go out of style decades ago?' It was a genuine and honest question that may be in the minds of many more good Christians. The truth is that fasting and prayer are needed today more than ever if we are serious about harvesting a community of people who will be transformed and get excited about the mission of God. The combination of fasting and praying is not a fad or a novelty but a spiritual discipline for all believers of all ages throughout the centuries and across the world.

'Didn't fasting and prayer go out of style decades ago?'

The Bible taught about both fasting and praying, and gave us commands to do both. The Bible also gives examples of people who fasted and prayed, using different types of fasts for different reasons, and all of which had very positive results. Jesus fasted and prayed. Jesus' disciples fasted and prayed after the Resurrection. Many of the Old Testament heroes and heroines of the faith fasted and prayed. The followers of John the Baptist fasted and prayed. Many people in the early church fasted and prayed. What the Scriptures have taught us, both directly and by the examples of the saints, is that this is something we are to do.

The harvest of transformed communities across our nation requires a breakthrough in the realm of the Spirit. Fasting and prayer break the yoke of bondage and bring about a release of God's presence, power and change. Our mission becomes God's mission when it begins in the crucible of prayer and fasting. I have seen this borne out in the course of my ministry and in the growth of our church. I have learned that fasting strengthens prayer as iron whets the sword. This is why 30,000 parishes of the denomination that I belong to, dedicate every February to prayer and fasting for their communities. At my church (Jesus House London) we also add the month of June. These are, of course, in addition to other days regularly taken out to pray and fast during the week as a seed sown towards the harvest of a transformed community.

The more seriously we approach prayer and fasting, the more serious the results we will experience in our missional journey. A spiritual fast involves our hearts and the way in which we relate and trust God. It relates to discerning and receiving strength to follow through what God might reveal to us about circumstances in our lives or a direction we are to take in making a difference in our communities.

When we fast, we are suddenly aware of what is good and evil. We have a heightened awareness not only of God's goodness and of God's commandments, but of the evil that abounds in the world around us. We experience a greater discernment of good and God seems to give us an opportunity to take a look again at our lives and the world around us, and to discern his will and purposes as we partake in his mission. The true harvest is not only a celebration of produce within a season but it is in a continuous transformation of souls in our communities for Jesus through the seed of praying and fasting and taking control in the spiritual realm.

Agu Irukwu is the Senior Pastor at Jesus House, London.

The more seriously we approach prayer and fasting, the more serious the results we will experience in our missional journey. A spiritual fast involves our hearts and the way in which we relate and trust God.

How Did I Get This Busy?

Meditation for the perplexed

Abbot Christopher Jamison

Life is busy but many of us speak as though 'being busy' is a force beyond our control. I have taken to asking people who come to the monastery where they find sanctuary in their life, meaning a sacred space or a place of refuge, and many say they find none. To reach out to our communities effectively, to be able to offer them the hope that is so often lacking today, we need to first be finding that hope for ourselves from God. That doesn't mean you have to spend hours every week on a retreat but finding time for stillness and silence in our everyday lives is vital to our connection with our creator. Simple meditation techniques that can be practised when alone or going about your day, are just one way to make space for sanctuary in your life and to open yourself up to hearing the voice of God.

> Many of us speak as though 'being busy' is a force beyond our control.

The monastic tradition offers two ways to help us in the silent times: the use of a repeated phrase, and the slow reading of sacred texts. Here we will look at the use of the repeated phrase. Such use was commended strongly by the desert fathers; it was their portable, internal sanctuary. When being still and silent it kept their distracting thoughts at bay; when they were working, it helped to turn the work into prayer. One favourite phrase of the first monks was 'O God, come to my assistance; O Lord make haste to help me.' This phrase which is taken from the Psalms, can be spoken individually, repeated internally or said communally when Christians gather to pray.

In solitude, the phrase, or a similar one, can be spoken in time with breathing rhythmically: 'O God, come to my assistance' as you breathe in, and 'O Lord make haste to help me' as you breathe out. The rhythm of this helps to lift you out of yourself and away from the noises in your head. If those distractions become insistent, one way to handle them is to pause from the phrase, consider the distraction (if it's important, write it down for attention later) and then consciously say to yourself you are putting it aside. If you combine this repeated use of a phrase with the advice on fixing times of silence in your day, then gradually the phrase enters your soul, starts to overflow into your day and begins to transform your perception of life.

Within the Christian tradition there is also the Jesus Prayer that is so popular in the Orthodox Churches of south-eastern Europe and Russia. This prayer involves the constant repetition of the phrase 'Lord Jesus Christ, have mercy on me, a sinner', to be said inwardly at all times of the day and night.

Other techniques can also help you prepare the body: sit four square (in the lotus position or on a chair with your limbs uncrossed), keep your neck and back straight, breathe deeply a few times. All these can prepare the body for what is not an art of relaxation but an art of concentration. Imagine you are preparing to hear something very important from somebody important: you would automatically uncross your legs, sit up and concentrate.

Prayer, therefore, should be short and pure.

In meditation, preparing your mind and body is done not as a mental and physical exercise but primarily to allow you to speak to God and finally to let God speak to you. Once I am speaking to the divine 'you' then anything can happen, and usually does, so let the conversation flow freely. The aim is purity of heart. St Benedict said, 'We must know that God regards our purity of heart and tears of compunction, not our many words. Prayer, therefore, should be short and pure' (Rule of St Benedict, 20:3–4). Benedict does not see a single prayer or mantra as the whole of prayer. He insists rather on the need for community life and community prayer as the essential framework for promoting prayer in its various forms, the many ways by which the diverse individuals come to address God as 'you'. This freedom of spirit within a framework is something that anybody can replicate in their life: you need a framework for your meditation, but let prayer flow freely within it.

I hope that you will find these simple techniques helpful as you seek God's inspiration for your HOPE for Harvest activities and for the life of your community. I pray that you will find sanctuary for yourself from the busyness of everyday life so that as God's spirit flows, the hope he places in you will overflow to all you meet.

A fuller account of this approach can be found in the author's best-selling book Finding Sanctuary – Monastic Steps for Everyday Life *(Orion, 2010).*

Christopher Jamison is President of the International Commission on Benedictine Education. He was formerly Abbot of Worth Abbey.

I pray that you will find
sanctuary for yourself from
the busyness of everyday life.

Daily Thankful Prayer

Abbot Jamison has encouraged us through a spiritual meditation to listen and to connect to God on a regular basis. Let us consider putting this into practice during the harvest season, focusing on the words of Luke 10:2 which say: *'The harvest is plentiful, but the workers are few. Ask the Lord of the harvest, therefore, to send out workers into his harvest field.'*

- Find a place to be still for a few minutes.
- Use a prayer as you breathe in and out, e.g. 'O God, come to my assistance' as you breathe in, and 'O Lord make haste to help me' as you breathe out.
- Listen: read through Luke 10:2 slowly and stop to reflect on any word or phrase which stands out. What is the Holy Spirit saying to you?
- Meditate: repeat reading this verse once or twice allowing time to reflect on what is being highlighted. What is God saying to you in this?
- Pray: then turn to prayer, offer back to God what you are discovering and talk to God about all that he is showing you in this verse and how this impacts others.
- Contemplate: from prayer move to stillness and rest in God's presence remaining open to his love.
- Finish by saying 'O Lord fill me with your love' as you breathe in and 'O God guide me today' as you breathe out.

Find a place to be still for a few minutes.

The challenge of Luke 10:2 is recognising that we are living in a time when the harvest is plentiful but that there are not enough workers. So let us pray for ourselves and for our churches that as we go out into our workplaces and communities we might be:

- Full of God's compassion and love so we might seek the harvest of people's souls.
- Generous with our hearts and lives.
- People who overflow with thankfulness for all that God has done for us, and we would be motivated by that to reach others with his love.
- A church that sees all the opportunities in our work and community to share the love of God through our words and actions.
- People who know God's hope and share it with those around us.

A Theology of Harvest

Revd Dr Gordon Gatward, OBE

The simple act of eating can link us to the agricultural world and the source of our food. As soon as you sit at a meal or pick up a snack you are in a position to appreciate the goodness and generosity of God on the one hand and the vulnerability and fragility of human life on the other.

> It is too easy for us to see creation as a source of wealth, there for us to exploit.

In Scripture, an abundance of food, the mark of a bumper harvest, is cause for rejoicing and celebration expressed in thanks to God, feasting and fellowship (see 2 Chronicles 30:22 and Zechariah 8:19). A shortage of food caused by the failure of the crops served as a reminder of our dependency on God, the consequences of God's people defying him and going against his will (Deuteronomy 8:11–20). Unfortunately today these latter consequences are too often suffered by the vulnerable poor whilst the guilty parties, those who are both profligate and prosperous, continue to follow their destructive path.

It is too easy for us to see creation as a source of wealth, there for us to exploit to our own ends instead of appreciating that we too are part of that creation. We can believe that the harvest is achieved through human knowledge, skill and effort imposed by the dominant and superior part of creation on all other parts, rather than acknowledging that the harvest is the result of our working in partnership with God, in tune with the rest of creation and as stewards under God's authority. Rather than rejoice and give thanks for the abundance of their food, many use it as an excuse for gluttony and obesity, often with little thought for the nature or history of what's being eaten or its value. The attitude is exactly that of the Deuteronomic world in which the giver and the gift of the harvest were ignored.

Similarly, the Scriptural imperative to provide food and hospitality for those less fortunate can be conveniently forgotten. Ezekiel 34 is frequently interpreted in terms of a prophetic condemnation of the religious elite who ignored the spiritual needs of the people. But the prophet's words can be as easily applied to those who, having plenty of food, gorge themselves whilst ignoring the plight of the billion children and adults who today go hungry.

Whilst Scripture says much about the physical agricultural harvest it also uses the image of the harvest to great effect. The resulting judgement for sin is often described in harvest terms such as when Jesus told the parable of the wheat and weeds in

Matthew 13. Jesus also uses that same imagery, however, to speak of the possibility of change, of the effect that the gospel of God's grace and forgiveness can have on people's lives (Matthew 9:36–37, Luke 10:2 and John 4:35). Harvest, which is the cause of hope in terms of satisfying physical hunger, is also a powerful image of how God's grace answers that spiritual emptiness that afflicts humanity. Through the sowing of that grace in human life and experience, relationships are transformed – with each other, with the rest of creation and above all with God. There is a glorious harvest as God's purposes come together, as the seed of grace bears its fruit of love, joy and peace. It's hardly surprising, therefore, that this is one of the images Jesus uses to portray the dawning of the kingdom, when all is fulfilled and God's purposes are fully achieved (Mark 5:26–29). The other image that he uses to describe the coming of the kingdom of God is that of a banquet (Matthew 22:1–10 and Luke 14:15–24). In this the harvest as a time for feasting, celebration and, above all, thanksgiving, fully becomes the symbol of both physical and spiritual blessing.

Gordon Gatward is Director of The Arthur Rank Centre, a Christian charity serving the spiritual and practical needs of the rural Christian community.

There is a glorious harvest as God's purposes come together, as the seed of grace bears its fruit of love, joy and peace.

THANKFULNESS

Thanksgiving as a Lifestyle

Pastor Agu Irukwu

By counting my blessings one at a time, it always amazes me what the Lord has done!

Although the harvest festival is an annual treat, giving thanks or living in a continuous state of thankfulness no matter what, is meant to be a way of life for Christians. Thanksgiving to me is simply an act of giving thanks to God through my actions. It is an outward expression of an inner gratitude. Feelings of gratitude are often displayed or expressed through clapping, dancing, singing and acts of generosity. That we of an Afro-Caribbean heritage might prefer to express our thanksgiving with energetic and exuberant gestures does not make our thanksgiving any more valuable than anyone else's. Acceptable gratitude is simply that which is offered with a grateful heart. Either in good times or bad times, looking inward on God's goodness fills my heart with gratitude. It is not impossible that one may easily forget the goodness of God in the hustle and bustle of daily survival. However, by counting my blessings one at a time, it always amazes me what the Lord has done! It is a helpful reminder that there is always something to be thankful about. Life is a gift so we should acknowledge that even our very next breath is something we should thank God for.

As we celebrate the harvest season through thankfulness and generosity, perhaps it is worth reminding ourselves why we must give thanks and also live a life of gratitude to God.

I give thanks because it is, first and foremost, a command by God: 'Give thanks in all circumstances,' Saint Paul tells the Thessalonian believers, 'for this is God's will for you in Christ Jesus.' A few years ago when my wife passed away after a period of sickness, it was challenging for me to live out this biblical text. But each time the awareness that the situation could have been worse comes to my heart, I am humbled to give thanks and be gracious to others.

Thanksgiving is also a sign of my dependence on, and trust in, God. When I stand before the congregation to testify of a blessing, as we often do in the Black churches, in addition to it being an act of thanksgiving, I am openly professing my total dependence on the Creator, without whom there would have been no blessing to testify to. Paul's letter to the Colossians encouraged them to be rooted, built up, established in their faith but abounding and overflowing in thanksgiving. A dependence on God that also echoes thanksgiving is Paul's letter to the Ephesians, reminding them to give thanks at all times and for everything. I have often said that thanksgiving is a protocol to be observed when approaching God in prayer. If people remember when we say 'thank you', surely God remembers when we say 'thank you', whether that thanks is expressed through generosity, outward confession or some other display. Psalm 100:4 *(The Message)* even talks about entering God's presence with the password 'Thank you!'.

Thanksgiving is an expression of my Christian identity, declaring that God is all in all and that my life is not my own. Understandably, it is hardly the lifestyle choice for our thriving twenty-first-century individualism. It is also not surprising that thanksgiving is not abundant in a world of poverty, oppression, tyranny, disease and death. But as I said, there is still much to be thankful for. And, as Paul said to the Philippians, we are called not to be anxious about anything but in every circumstance we should pray and make our requests with thanksgiving to God. The outcome for such a thankful heart is that anxiety is gone and replaced with God's peace.

At Jesus House, where I am a pastor, and across the 460+ churches of the Redeemed Christian Church of God that I oversee in the UK, we dedicate the first Sunday of every month as a thanksgiving day. It's always a special day to show our gratitude to God by bringing our gifts as an offering, similar to bringing harvest produce during the harvest season, with an outward display of praise and appreciation to God. For me, thanksgiving is in essence an integral part of my Christian DNA. I cannot be a Christian without being a thanks-giver! My contentment flows from who I am: a Christian. I am thankful that whereas I had been alienated from God, as Saint Paul reminds the believers in Ephesus, I am now a child of God, born anew into his kingdom by grace through the power of the Holy Spirit. With John Newton I can sing, giving thanks that I was blind, but now I see; I was lost but now have been found. I am content to rejoice in the gracious providence of such eternal treasure. That is more than enough to be thankful for!

So I am determined I will not wait for the autumn to celebrate harvest and neither will I wait for the Christian calendar to determine my gratitude to God. I will thank God daily for my family, my health, my trials, my success, my tears, my laughter and everything which makes me and matures me. I will celebrate harvest continually, irrespective of seasons and time of the year.

'For All That Has Been, Thanks!'

The Rt Revd Paul Bayes

As a young Christian, looking for followers of Jesus who might be my role models, I came across the Swedish diplomat Dag Hammarskjöld. He lived his life to the full as a politician and peacemaker, eventually becoming the Secretary-General of the United Nations in the fifties and early sixties. Alongside that he followed Jesus faithfully, writing down his spiritual journey in a book, *Markings*, that was published after he died.

His book is full of striking thoughts and phrases, but the one that has always stuck with me is very simple: 'For all that has been – thanks! For all that will be – Yes!'

As with harvest, so with all of life. Lightness and courage come as we say thank you.

Hammarskjöld had a full, active, complicated life, and he needed courage and strength. In the end he was killed in Africa, while on a peacekeeping mission. He received the Nobel Peace Prize after his death. It was a life full of achievement and struggle. But what kept him going, patiently working and praying for peace, was his sense of thanksgiving. He saw the world and all the beauty of it as a gift from God – but he also saw the difficulties and challenges of his work as a gift, and he was grateful for the chance to make a difference. In the light of his thanksgiving, he could say 'Yes!' to whatever God brought him for the future.

As a young man I wanted to be like that. I still do. A life rooted in thanksgiving is a life that can say 'Yes' to whatever God brings. That's why harvest thanksgiving is spiritually so important. It's too easy to take our food and warmth and wealth for granted. If we do, we will be resentful and defensive if our comfort is shaken.

But if we thank God for what we have then we free ourselves from slavery to it. It's God's, and he has given it to us. As with harvest, so with all of life. Lightness and courage come as we say thank you.

Paul Bayes is the Bishop of Hertford.

Thankfulness and Peace

Hanna Bullock

Since I was a young girl I was taught to give thanks for my dinner, to be grateful for the roof over my head and so, of course, I am grateful for these things. But when life gets tough, the 'be grateful for what you have' statement seems like just another cliché to live up to. It is not until I went through a season of anxiety and disappointment that the power of thankfulness really hit home for me. I was desperate for God's peace and this is what he said:

> Do not be anxious about anything, but in everything, by prayer and petition, with thanksgiving, present your requests to God. And the peace of God, which transcends all understanding, will guard your hearts and your minds in Christ Jesus (Philippians 4:6–7).

This is such a familiar verse but it's not until I read it at a time I was so desperate for God's peace and looking for something practical to grab hold of, that the words 'with thanksgiving' jumped out at me. I understood the importance of thankfulness in a completely different way: linked firmly with God's peace. I started to thank God for the things I knew were true. They were simple things that I had been taking for granted but as I thanked God for them I found that, little by little, his peace, which truly does go beyond all understanding, started to gain territory in my heart. I could feel my priorities shifting and could sense God's beautiful peace. Through this I have found thankfulness to be such an amazing tool to release his peace. I just needed to take the first step and start thanking him for what he'd already done and given me before worrying about my present and future needs.

Let the peace of Christ rule in your hearts . . . And be thankful (Colossians 3:15).

Hanna is a teaching assistant and photographer based in Hertfordshire.

Let the peace of Christ rule in your hearts ... And be thankful.

Feasting with Friends

Revd Joanne Cox

Autumn is my favourite time of the year. It promises crisp mornings, stunning sunsets and the glittery promises of the Christmas season to come. As the dark days help us travel into the reflections of a year drawing to a close, autumn offers the opportunity to take thankfulness seriously.

I have been fortunate enough to have grown up in a world where the American festival of Thanksgiving has grown in popularity (in no small part due to the TV sitcom Friends and their almost routine annual Thanksgiving catastrophes!). Thus, for me, thankfulness, thanksgiving and generosity all become associated with the smell of cinnamon spice, pumpkin pie and the clamour of dozens of people crowding into my house on cold wintery nights.

We use Thanksgiving (the third Thursday in November), to invite the hungry, the hopeless, local students and CEOs to share around a single table all the things that the previous year has brought them – the good, the bad and the ugly (the memories, not the people!). As we name these things together, the hospitality of the laden table before us helps us to remember that we are called to be people who offer the hospitality and generosity of the heart as well as the home.

As we feast together, we do so having first feasted on the word of God – words that tell us to 'give thanks in all circumstances, for this is God's will for you in Christ Jesus' (1 Thessalonians 5:18). We offer sentences and prayers of thanks to God for all that we have received over the past year, and we begin to dream about the possibilities to be hope-filled and generous throughout the year to come.

What are you thankful for today? What glimpses of the kingdom has God given you today? And how does this help you to become a person of great generosity, offering hospitality of home and of heart?

Joanne Cox is Evangelism in Contemporary Culture Officer for the Methodist Church and member of the HOPE Leadership Team.

What do We Deserve?

Dan Wilton

For me, the first step towards true thankfulness is realising just how little we deserve.

Just look around you right now. You see your hand? There are a ridiculous number of atoms just sitting there, making up your hand. Try jumping. I bet my entire piggy bank and all my A levels that you landed! Gravity still works last time I checked. Do we deserve to have the entire laws of science crafted and shaped to enable our very existence? Not a chance! Did God do it anyway? Yep.

More importantly, do we deserve eternal salvation at the price paid by Jesus? No and we never could. God knows that and yet he did it anyway. Feeling thankful yet?!

Even on an earthly scale, we are privileged practically beyond belief: food, clean water and shelter are not things we ever really question, yet to so many they are scarce and make the difference between life and death. When we realise how much we have compared to so many, then we have got to be thankful. Too often, though, we can fall into the trap of having the right attitude, but failing to act upon it. Thankfulness is not merely an attitude; it must be shown in our actions. True thankfulness is saying to God, 'Thank you for all you've given to me . . . how may I use it best to serve you?' If that means giving it all away, then so be it. At the same time, if we aren't thankful in the first place, then any actions we do are empty and lifeless: attitude is essential.

Realising how little we deserve is the first step; what you do next is between you and God. So let's go and change the world, one thankful heart at a time.

Dan is 18 years old and hoping to study theology at university.

> Let's go and change the world, one thankful heart at a time.

My Journey of Gratitude

Thandi Haruperi

Almost 13 years ago, I got news that changed my outlook on life. 'The test results have come back,' the doctor said. 'The HIV test, unfortunately, has come back positive.' I sat there in stunned silence trying to decipher the news; the word 'positive' is supposed to be good, so why did his look suggest otherwise?

He gave me a good prognosis, assuring me that my life chances were very high. With good HIV treatments available, people with HIV are living longer, healthier and more normal lives. In my case, with no symptoms or illness, a good immune system and a very low amount of virus in my body, I would not need to start treatment immediately and perhaps for a while to come. These were perhaps some of the benefits of being tested early.

What followed was a period of unanswered questions, bouts of shame, confusion and soul searching. Paradoxically, this was also the beginning of a personal journey that awakened me to my identity, my values and my purpose, enabling me to define and recreate myself into the person I wanted to be. Whilst some might have expected me to crawl away and hide until I shrivelled away like a fallen orange under my hot African sunshine, looking back now the only thing that has shrivelled in me is *fear*. Like a worm buried deep under the rubbish tip, I wriggled myself up and out.

The question people asked me is how I have managed to have peace and forge ahead in life despite this challenge. The apostle Paul's letter to the Philippians gave me a model that I have followed: first, not to be anxious about anything (which includes the bad news) but instead to pray and present my request to God. The caveat for me is the word 'thanksgiving' which has formed the foundation for my prayer and the outcome of my prayer. Paul was right: it is in my continuous thanksgiving that I have found the peace of God which transcends all natural knowledge and understanding. It is in thanksgiving that I have found sanity and it is thanksgiving and a grateful heart that has kept me going for 13 years since my diagnosis and will keep me going for many more years to come.

Thandi is the founder and director of RestorEgo, a consultancy which seeks to address various health related issues. She is an international speaker, an advocate, educator, mentor and advisor.

The Changing Harvest

Paul Farrington

I remember an autumn time when I was younger, I can nearly smell it. I remember early starts, the rising sun, lemonade, jam sandwiches and Kit-Kats. I stood with my dad on top of a large stack of straw bales, on a trailer moving down the fields of the farm. Bales were being thrown up by farm hands, family, friends and anybody else available. Harvest was a defined time; it had parameters and boundaries. There was a start and a finish.

How harvest time has changed! Farms are mechanised and computerised. They have more crops, with all year harvesting and seasons that drift into one. The world has got faster and faster and it appears there's nothing we can do about it! Sound familiar? Especially in these current times of uncertainty, life doesn't always feel defined. This isn't just in farming but is a reflection of the world in which we now live. Currency buys us less, pension funds grow smaller, jobs are not for life (though sometimes they may feel like a life sentence!), there is chaos on our streets and the finish line of retirement has moved. People still live in poverty, slavery still exists, wars still continue, earthquakes and natural disasters seem commonplace . . .

What did God originally intend these to be used for and look like?

When I focus on all the awful things in the world, I find it difficult to be thankful to God and generous towards others. So when I get overwhelmed I go for walks in the Lake District, read Psalm 23 and look at what God has entrusted to me: land, property, crops, machinery and my relationships with my farm hands, customers, suppliers, family and friends. Then I think, 'What did God originally intend these to be used for and look like?' There is a Hebrew word for this, *tshuva*, which basically means to return to God's original intention.

Maybe this harvest is the time to be truly thankful for what God has entrusted to us, to see what is in our hand, its original God intention, and how it can bless others, in our communities and around the world. In a time when harvest and abundance appear in short supply, may we as the UK church be a people where God's grace and his amazing provision are most evident. This harvest let's remember he can do more than we could ever ask or imagine, and ask him to reveal his *tshuva* for our lives and all he has blessed us with.

Paul is a farmer in Preston.

Thankfulness

Carl Beech

I'm one of the wealthiest people on the planet and that's a fact. Sure, Bill Gates, Warren Buffet, Carlos Slim and Laksmi Mitall could all write out a bigger cheque than me, and their huge wealth may make me feel poor by direct comparison, but it's still true that I'm incredibly wealthy because I live in the West.

God made me, knit me together, knows every day planned for me.

I also have a huge amount of choice. When I go to a supermarket to buy something simple, like yoghurt, it's not a simple task. There isn't just yoghurt any more. There's yoghurt with or without bits, there are subtle flavour mixtures, low fat or full cream versions, pro-biotic, authentic Greek, fake Greek. If you go to India you'll just find 'yoghurt'. It's a bit embarrassing when you stop to think about it. We have so much and it's easy to take for granted. Sometimes I find myself moaning about the traffic then I realise I am heading home in a comfortable car, listening to music playing via my iPod, connected to my car stereo. Perhaps our 'thankfulness' factor is being numbed and blunted by our wealth and our choices. We need to fight harder to get some perspective on how much we have. Sure we thank God for our health (superbly taken care of in the West) or for the food on our tables but a brother or sister in Christ somewhere around the world is praying for rain or for a cup of rice.

I like Psalm 139. It's not a typical harvest text but it reminds me of this: that God made me, knit me together, knows every day planned for me and every word on my tongue before I say it. It tells me that there is nowhere I can go where God 'isn't'. It tells me that God is sovereign and that everything I have (and I truly mean everything) comes from him. I'm in awe when I think that every breath I take and every thought and opinion I have is purely because of his grace. He sustains me nanosecond by nanosecond, instant by instant. Should he choose to, he could snuff me out like a candle in the wind.

So let's get back to basics. God is our provider, our sustainer and our life-giver. The one to whom we owe everything, from an English strawberry pro-biotic full-fat yoghurt to the very breath you just took. Let's remember how much we have and choose to be thankful this harvest.

Carl is General Director of Christian Vision for Men (CVM) and is on the councils of Evangelical Alliance, Fusion and Restored.

Thankfulness No Matter What

Sophie Cox

In some aspects of my life I have really found it hard to be thankful. I have a condition known as spinal muscular atrophy which means I have very limited muscle use and can no longer walk. I struggled with my condition when I was younger, comparing myself to other kids my age and wondering why I had this 'thing'. It seemed so unfair. I can't have a lot of spontaneity in my life, everything has to be organised to the last detail and I am limited in what I can do and where I can go. The doubts and anger led me away from God; I couldn't see how I could believe and trust in him one hundred per cent when I was going through things like spinal operations, my wheelchair breaking down over and over again, and dealing with the fact that I was prevented from doing most of the things I wished to do.

As I've grown older (I am now 23) of course I still feel this sometimes, but I've learnt to appreciate what is good in my life. I have incredible family and friends, I have my own flat, I can drive and I've been to some amazing places. I know now how much I really have to be thankful for. I have recently joined a new church where I have met gracious, helpful and caring people. I appreciate now that God has given me a great life and every day I pray a prayer of thanks. No matter what, I know deep down I'm really lucky. Yes there will be challenges of course, but without those I would never grow and become stronger. Sometimes I ask my friends what they think I'd be like if I was 'normal' and they just simply reply, 'Well, you wouldn't be you,' and I think that says it all.

Sophie Cox graduated from the University of Northampton in 2010 and is a freelance photographer who is also currently training as an independent financial advisor.

Medics Under Pressure

Dr Janet Goodall

'I've just about had enough. I'm getting out!' How many times have we heard this? How often have we thought it? In Britain, we so often hear of stress, burnout and post-traumatic stress disorder. Healthcare professionals are not the only ones to witness one tragedy too many or simply to suffer from being overstretched. Yet if we lived in a war zone or a part of the world affected by natural or unnatural disasters, we might then consider our British trials to be relatively modest.

In his incarnation Jesus, too, suffered fatigue. At times, he felt quite overwhelmed by the horror that lay ahead of him, but received grace and strength to go through with it. He knew the fullest force of temptation because he never yielded, and therefore he now knows exactly how we feel when we are tempted to give in, give up or get out.

When Paul was persuaded to leave Ephesus, he knew that arrest and possible death lay ahead but still he longed to complete his appointed task. Much of what he says in his letter to the young Ephesian church is still relevant and encouraging to those working under pressure today. He reminds us of our calling, our competencies and the character God has in mind for us.

Whether we are in our consulting rooms, operating suites or committee meetings, there is the church.

Even though he was writing from prison, Paul quickly turns to praise. He lists the many blessings given to those who, through Jesus Christ, have been adopted into his family, chosen by God with the thrice-mentioned intention that they should live to his praise and glory. This repetition should make us ask if that is how we come across – not only when wearing our shining going-to-church faces, but also in the workplace. The church is the body of Christ, not just a building. So, whether we are in our consulting rooms, operating suites or committee meetings, *there* is the church. God is bringing all things under the headship of Christ so this must include everything that happens in our places of work. Therefore, our ultimate authority is not our own autonomy, primary care trust, health authority, or even the Minister of Health, but Christ himself. Assurance that all new edicts, difficult patients and ethical dilemmas are to be dealt with 'to the praise of his glory' should help us to look trustfully to God for the wisdom and understanding 'lavished' on us for times like these, rather than letting ourselves get anxious, frustrated and exhausted. Paul's own great enthusiasm would have been fuelled by knowing that the Greek *en theo* means 'possessed by a god'. If our calling is to be possessed by the God of gods, then we too should work with enthusiasm.

This is an extract from an article written by Dr Janet Goodall, an Emeritus Consultant Paediatrician and a member of the Christian Medical Fellowship, based on a talk on Ephesians by Canon Mark Brown at a CMF day conference.
To read the full article visit:
www.cmf.org.uk/publications/content.asp?context=article&id=1840

God is bringing all things under the headship of Christ so this must include everything that happens in our places of work.

WORK

A Celebration of Work

Mark Greene

Thanksgiving, harvest and work

Harvest was traditionally a time to celebrate the firstfruits of crops that had been grown. Here in twenty-first-century UK the firstfruits of most of our labours are no longer new potatoes in March, bushels of barley in August or boxes of Bramleys in late September. Around 530,000 people are still involved in farming but, for the rest of us, work means things like cleaning offices, making deliveries, writing software, serving meals and delivering lessons. The rewards of our labour and the provision God makes for us are usually the wage that comes weekly or monthly and we may see this as the main fruit of our work. Biblically, however, work, cannot be reduced to just an instrument for provision. God's intentions for work are much richer and broader. Work is central to his mission – a key component in fulfilling the Abrahamic promise to bless others, a key context for seeing God's ways lived out – thy will be done on earth as it is in heaven. In sum, a primary arena for mission in the broadest sense.

Thanking God for work

It can be hard, it can be exhausting, it can be exhilarating, it can be fun . . . but work is one thing everyone has to do whether it's at home, in school, at church, in the office, in the field or in a factory. In fact, as Genesis 2:15 tells us, we were created to work. God, the worker God, who planned, implemented, finished, reviewed and celebrated his own work of creation, gave humankind purposeful, creative work to do: 'The LORD God took the man and put him in the Garden of Eden to work it and take care of it.'

Tragically, Adam and Eve rebelled against God and that rebellion had consequences for work: enter toil, drudgery and futility. Nevertheless, purposeful, productive work is still part of God's plan for us and work can still be the source of many, many joys and satisfactions. There's the joy of getting a job done, of working with other people, using a skill, being creative, solving a problem, developing a product or service that makes someone's life just a little better, cleaning a street so that disease doesn't spread, serving a coffee with the kind of smile that makes someone want to come back the following day . . .

Thank God for such opportunities.

Of course, we all do a lot of work that isn't paid but which still contributes enormously to people's lives: babies fed, beds made, homes decorated, ingredients turned into nutritious, delicious meals, hedges cut, cars washed and so on. There is joy in that just as there is also joy in being paid so that we can feed, clothe, house, educate, treat those we are responsible for. There is the joy of having money to give to God, to give to those in need, to help someone along a good path, or up from a fall, or simply to put a big smile on someone's face . . .

The workplace is the single biggest mission field we have.

Thank God for such opportunities.

God uses work in other ways too – to develop and hone our talents and skills in the service of others, to learn to do all we do in his strength, not just in our natural abilities, and to learn to do whatever we do 'with all your heart, as working for the Lord, not for men, since you know that you will receive an inheritance from the Lord as a reward. It is the Lord Christ you are serving' (Colossians 3:23–24).

Thank God for such opportunities.

Work is a central part of God's mission. There are some 29.14 million workers in the UK. The workplace is the single biggest mission field we have and for most of us it's the place where we spend the most time with people who don't know Jesus. It's the place where we already have relationships, and lots of them. The average person in work connects, talks to, writes to, meets with and emails at least 50 people a week. Some people – teachers, for example – may connect to hundreds in a week. Unlike some overseas mission fields, we don't have to figure out the culture, we don't have to learn the language or the jargon; we already know it. Furthermore, the workplace is the place where we see people in all kinds of situations – at their best and sometimes at their worst. It's the place they get to see us, too, and to see in what ways Jesus might be alive in our lives, to see what difference he makes to our work, to our response to rebuke and reward, to success and to failure, to pressure and to ease, to rivals and colleagues, to bosses and subordinates. It's the place we learn to grow in the fruits of the Spirit – love, joy, peace, patience, goodness, faithfulness, gentleness, kindness, self-control.

Thank God for such opportunities.

It's the place we get to bless people and minister to them in all kinds of ways – by doing good work on time, by going the extra mile, by encouraging others, by getting them a cup of coffee when they don't have time, or sharing a sandwich, by noticing if someone is down, by praying for them without them knowing, by offering to pray for them, by celebrating their successes and commiserating with their disappointments, by befriending the person no one else likes . . . In short, by showing love.

Thank God for such opportunities.

The workplace is the place we may get to stand up for truth and justice.

The workplace is also a place where God disciples us. Why wouldn't he? Why wouldn't he use our bosses and colleagues to teach us about pride and humility, about when to say 'yes' and when to say 'no'? Why wouldn't he use our everyday situations to prompt us to pray, to trust in his provision and in his timing? Why wouldn't he teach us to become people of our word in the workplace – to do what we say we will do when we say we will do it? Why wouldn't he teach us about learning to practise forgiveness and about learning to say sorry in the place where we spend over forty per cent of our waking lives? Why wouldn't he want to teach us, as he taught Joseph and Daniel, that he has wisdom for our work?

Thank God that he uses such opportunities.

The workplace may well also be the place where we learn perseverance and resilience, the place where day by day we are sharply aware that our values are not the same as other people's, where we feel like aliens and strangers, as Peter puts it in 1 Peter 2. It's the place where some, maybe most people around us will regard our trust in Jesus as odd, quaint, ridiculous, weird, stupid. It's the place where we may suffer because we believe there's no other way, no other truth and no other source of life. It's the place where our gracious Father may teach us to thank him for such opportunities to suffer for him.

Thank God.

The workplace is the place we may get to stand up for truth and justice – to go in to bat for a colleague who has been maligned, to challenge an unjust practice, to make sure that someone gets the bonus they deserve, or to nip some gossip in the bud.

Thank God for such opportunities.

It's the place we get to share good news as well as show it. It won't happen every day or even every week but over time, as trust grows, the Lord often provides opportunities to testify to the difference that God makes in our lives: that he helped me get through that really difficult patch, that he helped me not bear a grudge against that colleague, that he helped me say 'sorry' to someone I'd offended, or indeed to testify that he helped me in the work itself, to do something better or faster than I have ever done it before or to do something really difficult – firing someone, going to tell a parent their child has been in an accident . . .

Thank God for such opportunities.

The workplace is the place where over time we may well also have an opportunity to share the gospel directly, to do some Bible study, to invite a colleague to Alpha or Christianity Explored or just out for a coffee with some Christian friends they may like. Again, it won't happen every day but, over time, as trust grows, as we pray and as the Spirit leads, God who is probably wooing our colleagues in a whole variety of ways may graciously grant us the opportunity to share the gospel.

Thank God for such opportunities.

There may be Christians from other churches in our workplace so there may be an opportunity to pray and work together in mission. Or we may be the only Christian but, either way, we should go to work as the individual representative of the body of Christ, supported, just like an overseas missionary, by the prayers, encouragement and wisdom of our brothers and sisters in our local church.

Thank God for such opportunities for God's people to work together.

In sum, the workplace isn't just a place where we can participate in God's rich and diverse mission; it's also the place where we can come to enjoy a richer relationship with him, to learn that he cares about everything we do and every aspect of our lives, to learn that he is interested in all of it and that we can talk to him about all of it, to learn that he is in us day by day, minute by minute, second by second and that he is with us. He is Emmanuel, God with us, day by day, minute by minute, second by second. May we have eyes to see and lips to testify.

Thank God for his lavish and extraordinary grace in, through and at work.

Mark Greene is the Executive Director of the London Institute for Contemporary Christianity.

The workplace isn't just a place where we can participate in God's rich and diverse mission; it's also the place where we can come to enjoy a richer relationship with him.

The Smell of Jesus

Simi Adedeji

The first breath Jesus took was that of a manger – the smell of the lonely, dispossessed, broken and the lost, the aroma of his calling. As he grew older he was found amongst them, loving them and teaching, and he said that whatever we do to the least of his brothers we do to him.

One day I took a wrong turn and found myself face to face with a heap of rags in Skid Row, LA. The smell that overwhelmed me was unmistakably human, yet it stung my eyes and tore at the back of my throat. I moved closer and saw a face peering from beneath the rags wreathed in a big smile. Then I felt ashamed. I was dressed to the nines in designer gear and wafting designer perfume and I suddenly felt dirty. I realised that I stank. I could smell my pride and my heart devoid of compassion. I remembered the words of Jesus Christ: 'I was hungry and you gave me something to eat . . . whatever you did for one of the least of these brothers of mine, you did for me.'

Here I was looking into the eyes of Jesus, a homeless man sleeping in a doorway. I stretched out my hand and said, 'Hello.'

He sat up and said, 'I love that accent; you're not from round here!'

I smiled, 'Oh yes, I am.' I stood there taking in the desolation and the poverty. 'This is where Jesus lives; this is where I want to be found.'

I now work in a magistrates' court, and the waiting rooms have a smell like the manger where Jesus was born. When the accused walk into the courtroom, they bring it in with them. I do not wrinkle my nose but I say a silent prayer for the discernment of the Holy Spirit in the decisions that I pass as judgements over their lives. I know Jesus is in the house, I can smell him. He stands with the least of his brothers and whatever judgement I pass on them I pass it on Jesus. I am always aware of the weight and effect the decisions that I make have on people's lives.

When I do meet Jesus, I don't want him to say, 'You're not from round here,' like the homeless man on Skid Row. I would expect a smile filled with recognition, a big hug and the words, 'You smell nice . . . you smell like me!' To be a Christian is one of the yuckiest jobs on the planet, but I am thankful for it and would not change it for all the diamonds in the world.

Simi sits as a magistrate on the Luton and South Bedfordshire Bench. She is a poet, political activist, a public speaker, a wife and a mother of three teenage girls and lives in Luton, Bedfordshire.

Value People Highly

Laurence Singlehurst

In recent years the importance of the workplace and how we as Christians can make a difference both where we work and how we work has come back onto the church agenda. Many of us long to make a difference through our values and the way we work and our Christian history tells us how. From the eighteenth century, pioneering Christians in the business world have made a difference by realising that people have a high value.

People are extremely valuable. It is at the heart of the Christian message because Christ died for all (2 Corinthians 5:14). This gives us a very powerful picture of how valuable people are. In the Old Testament we see that we are created in the image of God; in the New Testament we are told that Jesus died for us. For us!

A little bit of the kingdom of God has come to that previously lonely corner.

Samuel Budget, an eighteenth-century trader during the rise of Methodism, bought from people in a ruthless fashion and sold to people making maximum profit. He was then convicted that people actually had value and therefore he should buy from them so they could make a profit, and sell his good products at a fair price. His approach to business was embraced by Methodism, his story was published and his principles began to impact the world of commerce far and wide. We also have the wonderful examples of Sunlight Soap and Cadbury where business owners began to treat their workers with value and provide good salaries and good places to work. However, in recent years, through the pressures of commercialism and our consumer society, some companies that once held to these values now feel under pressure to slowly let them go. As individuals we can often get caught up in the competitiveness of our environments and we lose a sense of our colleagues' value and lose sight of the fact that the way we treat them is significant.

Imagine it this way: gardeners recognise that in the south-west corner of your garden you can create a micro climate; there is more sunshine if it is protected and you can grow plants in that corner that will only flourish there. When we go to work and value people we can influence maybe two desks to the left and the two desks to the right and create a micro climate. A friend of mine, Julie, started a new job and found the little corner she worked in wasn't very friendly. People only made cups of coffee for themselves, but when Julie made one, she asked if she could make a drink for anyone else at the same time. She brought in cakes for her birthday and, after one year, a relatively short time, a little bit more sunshine had come to that corner of her office. Julie's example changed the entire nature of that small community. Now everyone offers to make coffee, everyone brings cakes in on their birthday, and a little bit of the kingdom of God has come to that previously lonely corner.

Property developers are often seen as the shark of sharks, the toughest and meanest of the big fish that live in the city. In the seventies and eighties there was a highly successful firm of developers and their work always seemed to be good for the environment. They created buildings that were great to work in and that were priced at a fair price, yet everyone made a profit. They were called Hazelmere Estates and they were famous because they seemed in essence to place a high value on employees at the heart of their business. David Pickford, the MD at that time, was a Christian man who believed it was vital to treat people with value as well as make a profit, and he did both.

As we value people, we show them something of how God feels about them.

Many people have commented on the changes in the way people are now made redundant. Previously it might have been done by your boss or the owner of the company but now it seems to increasingly be the function of the HR department. It can be cold and clinical, and the human touch, the sense that each individual is valued, seems to have gone with it. This is a slow trend of seeing people as a widget in the system, with no value and dignity. Yet there are still companies that decide to do something different.

I did a carol service a number of years ago for a famous merchant bank who placed a high value on employees. They made it clear that no one would ever be made redundant by Human Resources or sacked by someone they didn't know. If, sadly, someone had to be let go, the news would always come from the people they worked for, redundancy or terms would be as generous as possible and therefore each person knew they were valued. Every Christmas, employees were given a free turkey and they could choose a small, medium or large one. If you chose large they suggested you bring a lorry! This company maintained, based on their Jewish tradition, that valuing people highly was a better way to do business. They could speak with some authority as they were, and still are, one of the most profitable banks in London. They did not find valuing people a problem but a bonus.

So as you and I go to work or meet our friends at the school gate, let us take this value with us. As we value people, we show them something of how God feels about them and how much they are worth to him. We may be the ones influencing company policy at a high level, we may be looking out for a friend or colleague who is having a difficult time, or simply offering to make others a coffee when we can. Whatever we do, as we value people, it will change everything.

Laurence Singlehurst is the Director of Cell UK.

Trusting God in Unemployment

Chris Smith

I was first made redundant early in 2010 then, shortly after finding another job, I was made redundant again in November of the same year. I have been unemployed since then, picking up a few odd days' work here and there, but finding nothing more secure or permanent. There are so many people out of work that employers can afford to be choosy. There's little incentive for them to take on someone who would need to learn certain aspects of a role when they can pick someone who has every single qualification they're looking for. This can make it really hard to even get an interview. Likewise, finding temporary work is getting harder and harder as there are so many people fighting over so few roles.

It has been a challenging and stretching time for me being unemployed, especially when, not long after my second redundancy, my wife and I found out we were expecting a baby. I've felt the added pressure of wanting to provide for my family, but being unable to find a job to make that happen. I've spent many hours looking for and applying for jobs and I've tried to keep myself in a routine so that I don't lose motivation and purpose. It can be hard spending so much of the day alone; it's easy to start feeling isolated and directionless. Reading the Bible and praying have become a key part of my day and God has been teaching me a lot through this difficult season. He's been reminding me that his timing is different to mine but he has purpose in the things that happen (even when they don't make much sense to me!). I know God wants the best for me and my family so I keep reminding myself of that when things are hard.

I've spent a lot of time worrying about what I needed to earn to pay the bills but gradually God has been reminding me that he has it all under control. He's provided for us in amazing ways and has been teaching us to trust in him. He's met all our needs – even providing a totally unexpected holiday for us that we could never have afforded ourselves. Of course it's hard not to worry when the bills come in or the car needs repairs, but I have to keep coming back to the fact that God hasn't let us down in the past and he will provide what we need.

Over the last year I have realised that God is far more interested in my character than my 'calling'. Because I've not been able to find my purpose in work, I've had to find it in God instead. I've been available to help out my wife during her pregnancy and the early days of our daughter's life, plus I've been able to offer more time to church and to friends. One time I was helping some friends move into their new home and felt like God said, 'Are you willing to be the answer to other people's prayers?' Sometimes it's easy to be caught up in the busyness of life and not make time to do the things that are important to God and to help other people.

I try to be optimistic when I think about the future. I would of course love to be back in a secure job (which I don't think I'd take for granted ever again!) and I have to trust that even though I can't see where the job will come from or when, *God will provide*. I've definitely learnt that this is a situation I can't control myself so I'm trying to keep myself fully surrendered to God and trust that he knows how it will all work out. I can't do this alone but 'I can do everything through him who gives me strength' (Philippians 4:13).

Chris lives in Watford with his wife Anna and their daughter Martha.

Sometimes it's easy to be caught up in the busyness of life and not make time to do the things that are important to God and to help other people.

Ideas for Equipping, Empowering and Affirming your Church in Their Daily Ministry

Mark Greene

There are loads of ways churches can celebrate the various workplaces of their congregation, supporting them on a Sunday (or in their small group) in their Monday-to-Friday missional work. The following ideas reflect how a rich engagement with work can express itself in a local church's gathered meeting. They explore how we can help create a healthy community consciousness of the primacy of daily work as missional service amongst our communities. Many of the ideas don't take very long, and cost absolutely nothing, but could make a real difference in how supported and encouraged people feel in their work.

Connecting Work and Harvest in Non-Rural Churches

Could be done in small groups

Since most people don't make their living by farming, traditional displays of bringing food into the church as offerings may remind us of God's provision of our daily bread, but they don't visually connect to the way that God has chosen to meet our people's material needs. A suburban child does not look at a display of potatoes and make the connection to their father's job in IT.

A contemporary harvest display might involve a range of objects that represent how people are engaged in work such as a hard hat, a baby's bottle, a set of keys, a spade, a computer or a syringe. In one church, the whole congregation were invited to bring an object that represented their work and then were invited to lay it on the altar as a symbolic dedication of their work, their co-workers and their workplaces to God. Children were involved and brought text books or pencils and one unemployed person laid their UB40 form on the altar – a moving reminder of their lack of paid work but also of God's provision through the wider community.

Another church asked people to bring in pictures of themselves in their workplaces and displayed them around the church, as a way for the community to get to know and appreciate the variety of places God has given them work.

TTT – This Time Tomorrow

During a normal Sunday worship service, perhaps once a month, the church leader interviews one of the congregation for two minutes. They ask the interviewee a few questions about their daily occupation, about what they will be doing TTT – 'This Time Tomorrow'. The questions can be really simple:

- What do you do?
- What are your challenges/the things you are thankful for?
- How can we pray for you?

Stories and prayer requests become part of the way the church does life together.

The interviewees do not need to be the Chief of Police, the CEO of IBM or the England fly half. In fact, even if you have some with an extraordinary role, it's usually best to start with people doing ordinary work in ordinary places, and to include people whose daily occupation may not be paid, such as a housewife, a retired person involved in a variety of purposeful activities, and those who are unemployed.

This simple practice tends to have a range of transformative benefits:

1. It acknowledges, affirms and honours the interviewee, telling them that what they do every day is important to the leader, important to the church and important to God.

2. As TTT follows TTT month by month, the whole congregation recognises ever more deeply that ordinary Christians doing ordinary things are important to God – even if some people never get to share from the front. These stories and prayer requests become part of the way the church does life together.

3. TTT creates new conversations. It gives people who didn't know the interviewee an easy way to talk to them, and perhaps to share similar challenges or pertinent insight or encouragement.

4. TTT triggers a new *kind* of conversation. Issues that are often considered to be off the spiritual agenda (work, futility, failure, success, daily relationships, mission in daily life) are validated as legitimate topics for conversation and prayer.

Consider:

- Once you've done the interview you could ask others to stand who share the same issues or pressures so they can also be prayed for.

- Getting creative in the way you do the interviews. One church arranged for members to use a small video camera to record their interviews in their workplace which naturally helped people understand each other's everyday contexts much better.
- Providing an opportunity for people to give testimony to how the congregation's prayers have been answered in future services.

Commissioning and Thankfulness

Also suitable for small groups

When someone gets a new job or is promoted it is something to be thankful for and perhaps to acknowledge as a whole church. Furthermore, a new job is not just a source of provision; it is an opportunity for mission and ministry so, in the same way that one would pray for a new pastor, it is hugely encouraging to commission someone for their new job or their new role.

Ideally, prayers might have three main thrusts:

- Reflect an understanding of the job to be done and how it may contribute positively to others, the place it will be done and the skills required.
- Reflect the conviction that the Christian goes into the workplace as a representative of the Lord Jesus, carrying his commission and confident in his promise to be 'with' his disciples 'to the very end of the age' (Matthew 28:19–20).
- Reflect the conviction that the Christian goes into the workplace as the individual representative of your church. Thank God that he has given your community an opportunity to make an impact in that place.

Opportunities for Prayer

After the offering

Most churches do this every week so you don't have to change anything in a service to begin to enrich people's understanding of God's generosity and the variety of ways he may bless his people in, at and through work, and other mechanisms of provision. Across a year you could probably teach and pray a whole theology of work, divine provision, money and generosity, just through offertory prayers. Themes might include:

- Gratitude for work.
- Gratitude for being created with skills.

- Recognition of the need for stewardship.
- Recognition of God as the source of money.
- Gratitude for money.
- Gratitude for the privilege of being able to give.
- Gratitude for our workplaces, our bosses and colleagues.

General prayer

The simplest way to build faith-consciousness is to include a reference to the world of work and school within general prayers. Take, for example, a confessional prayer like:

> Lord, we bring to you our relationships – our relationships at home, our relationships with neighbours, our relationships at work or at school. Show us where we have failed to love as you would have us love.

The simple addition of seven words 'our relationships at work or at school' instantly transforms this prayer into one that encourages the whole congregation to recognise that their life cannot be compartmentalised, that God is interested in the 9 to 5. It only takes another three seconds to say!

Prayer and the rhythm of the non-agricultural year

Plough Sunday, Rogation Sunday and harvest were key moments in the agricultural year that in a rural community everyone shared. In a mixed economy, however, there are still moments we all share. So, for example, for the bulk of the population the tax year begins in the first week of April, so the first Sunday of April might be a good moment to ask for God's blessing on the work of our hands in the coming year. Similarly, May Day retains some of its historic connection with work and therefore might be a natural moment to give thanks for our participation in God's mission through work.

There is no obvious equivalent to Plough Sunday but it might still be marked as Technology Sunday, as a moment when we thank God for the liberating impact of technology on our lives and its helpfulness in limiting drudgery and producing goods and services that contribute to human flourishing to the glory of God.

Indeed, many of the advances in the widespread use of technology have emerged out of a biblical understanding of work that sought to limit the drudgery imposed on people and animals. It's true of the development of the watermill – long known in the East – but only brought into widespread use by Benedictines seeking to reduce toil. It's true also of the clock, of the iron horseshoe, of the crank . . .

Prayer and pressure points

Just as Plough Sunday and Rogation Sunday and harvest represented key moments in the agricultural cycle – not least in terms of effort – so a church can connect its prayer for different people into the rhythm and pressure points of their working year – sheep farmers in lambing season, accountants at the end of the tax year, kids at exam time, teachers at the beginning and end of terms, shop assistants during sales. An example calendar is laid out on pages 44-45. There is a downloadable version on the HOPE and LICC websites www.hopetogether.org.uk and www.licc.org.uk and you can ask people in the church to fill it in and then perhaps display it.

Praying blessing at work

On the completion of each day's work of creation in Genesis 1 – 2 God blessed the living creatures he had made, bidding them increase and multiply and fill the earth. Blessing is powerful – our words matter! How can we bless our work?

Ask the congregation for aspects of their work that they would want to bless. Help them explore why it would be good to bless each aspect.

Possible areas:

- The privilege of having work.
- Relationships at work.
- The prosperity of the organisation for whom we work.
- Management and decision making.
- Use of resources.
- The 'output' of our hands and minds.
- The godly aspects of the culture and values of the organisation.
- Evangelism.

In groups of three or four ask them to construct a short prayer (one or two sentences) to bless one aspect of work. Record and group these.

As a congregation, pray blessing on work as different people stand up and read out their short prayers.

Type up the prayer of blessing to be circulated for future use.

> Blessing is powerful – our words matter! How can we bless our work?

God blessed the living creatures he had made, bidding them increase and multiply and fill the earth.

Praying for St Paul's at Work

Job	Jan	Feb	Mar	Apr	May	Jun	Jul	A
Plumber	■	■						
Builder				■	■			
Carpenter						■	■	■
Retail Assistant	■							
Accountant			■	■				
Taxi Driver								
Teacher	■					■	■	
Classroom Assistant	■		■			■	■	
HR Manager			■					
Receptionist								
Administrator			■			■		
Nurse	■	■						
Paramedic	■	■						
Solicitor			■	■				
Counsellor	■	■						
Police Officer	■					■	■	■

ep	Oct	Nov	Dec	St Paul's people
		■	■	Alex Carlisle, Jim Hanson, Laurence Cloake
				Robert Kingston, Josh Ewing, Pete Simpson
				Jack Cooper
	■		■	Kim Richardson, Sally Harris, Freddie Bowman
				Jean Crawford, Stephen Armstrong, Emily Smith
			■	Timothy Gray, Mark Greene
■			■	Pamela Fisher, Nicholas Cullen, Sarah Patley
■			■	Joe Quemby, Hannah Jarvis
■				Helen Gales
				Julie Fitzpatrick,
			■	Carly McDonnell, Rosie Barnes, Richard Adams
		■	■	Steve Howard, Wendy Taylor
		■	■	Cathy Ward,
■	■			Thomas Leyland, Louise Campbell, Anna Hughes
			■	Victoria Westwood
			■	Joanne Williams, Trevor Harding, Paul Jones

An example prayer of blessing

Thankfulness

Bless the Lord O my soul and forget not all his benefits. We bless You, Lord, for your gift of work – for the opportunity to co-labour with you and to provide for our families and communities.

Output

We bless the creativity and skills you have given which enable us to make goods and deliver services that others need.

Relationships

We bless every contact with another person, be they colleague, customer or supplier. We bless those we meet, speak to or email, that they may experience something of your love through us.

Resources

We bless the use and stewardship of all resources: financial, material and human. We bless ethical decisions in how we source our materials and how we dispose of waste.

Organisation

We bless the organisations for which we work; we bless them as employers and pray that job opportunities may multiply through them. We bless the management decisions to reflect kingdom values.

Culture

We bless the culture of our organisations. May they be contexts for human flourishing – places where people feel valued. We pray for people's lives outside of work – that they will be honoured.

Evangelism

We bless our contact with non-believers through work. We bless every opportunity to speak of you, through both our words and actions, with fruitfulness.

Amen.

We bless the creativity and skills you have given which enable us to deliver services that others need.

Praying for Businesses and Workplaces in Your Community

Also a great idea for small groups

Businesses are vital to alleviating poverty. People need help, food, medicine, shelter and stable honest government but they also need jobs.

One of the things a congregation can do is to thank God for the businesses, shops and organisations you have in your area. Proactively you could inform local shopkeepers or businesses that the church would be praying for their health and prosperity (Jeremiah 29:7) and ask them if they had any particular requests. In one small town, the pastor simply went into the local shops – but you could ask individual members of a congregation to do this or to adopt a shop/business that they used or was significant to them. This is also a great way of engaging in a local community.

Extra ideas:

- Come to church dressed in your workplace clothes.
- Bring examples of your work to church.
- Visit your congregation in their workplace.
- Invite local industries to make a display in church during harvest or celebrate what they do with a DVD about them including things to celebrate and things to pray for. Or invite local business people to come and represent their industry and thank them for their contribution to the community and pray for them. You could link up with a number of churches in the area to make sure different industries are honoured within your community.
- Run clinics for people in your church and community who are looking for work, offering help with CV writing, job applications and interview skills.
- Develop a church CD library with great resources for workers to listen to on their commute (or make your Sunday talks downloadable from your website and suggest links to other helpful podcasts).
- Have a map on the wall in your church, indicating where people are employed (much as you would a traditional missionary map of people around the world).

Small Groups in the Workplace

Over the years there have been a number of experiments on how Christians in the workplace can be supported and support one another in bringing purpose to what they do Monday to Friday 7 a.m. to 7 p.m.

One idea that has been tested over the years is called Bands where three or four people gather together (friends or acquaintances) and they have a loose structure based around three Ps.

They read a Bible verse and tell a story of what God has done in their lives.

The first P is **Presence**, they read a Bible verse and tell a story of what God has done in their lives since they last met and anything that brings a sense of Jesus into their gathering. They then go on to the second P which is **Pressure**. What pressures do they face as Christians in the workplace; what are their challenges at work, with family and in life? They pray for one another about the issues raised. The last P is **Purpose**. What are each of them trying to do in terms of being transformational, 'salt and light', in the way they work? They then pray for each other about their purpose and what they are hoping to see happen as they live out their Christian faith in their work space.

These groups can meet weekly, fortnightly, monthly or whatever suits the people involved. Using this easy format means they don't really need a leader and they can take place anywhere they can find a quiet corner whether that's in an office, a meeting room or a café.

RESOURCES

Supporting Christians at Work, **Mark Greene (LICC, 2001), £5**
A concise guide for pastors which sets out the vision, the theological foundations and provides a host of practical ideas for everything from preaching to groups to décor that can help create a worker-friendly church without distorting the rest of the church's work. Available from www.licc.org.uk .

The Heavenly Good of Earthly Work, **Darrell Cosden (Paternoster, 2006), £8.99**
Genuinely original book which makes the case for the eternal significance of our daily work. Tightly argued, important theological reflection.

Love Work, Live Life, **David Oliver (Authentic, 2006), £5.99**
David Oliver helps the reader explore ways to bring passion and vibrant spirituality to their work, whatever it is, making it a place that resonates with a sense of purpose and destiny.

The Christian Medical Fellowship (CMF) works to unite and equip Christian doctors, students and healthcare professionals. The fellowship brings together more than 4,000 doctors and 1,000 medical students, and links with around 70 similar bodies worldwide, www.cmf.org.uk.

Thank God it's Monday, **Mark Greene (SU, 2001), £6.99**
A fun, popular level book which includes material on theology of work, vocation, ministry, evangelism, ethical challenges and work-life integration.

SMALL GROUP RESOURCES

Christian Life and Work, **Mark Greene (LBC, 2000), £25**
A six-part 2-hour film includes a leader's guide keyed in to *Thank God it's Monday*.
Topics include: theology of work, evangelism, relating to the boss, truth-telling,
pressure, spirituality at work and work/life integration. Each session includes a
creative Bible reading, teaching, group exercises and commentary on the issues raised
from a check-out lady, a mechanic, a housewife, an IT clerk, a teacher and a company
director, www.licc.org.uk.

Life on the Frontline (LICC, 2012), £8
With six short films and discussion material for groups, the series explores how we
can help one another live fruitfully and faithfully for Christ in the ordinary, daily
places we live our lives, www.licc.org.uk.

I Love My Work, **Robin Scurlock and Steve Goss**
(Terra Nova, 2002), £6.99
Six studies for small groups preceded by a helpful exploration of the key issues for
leaders. Can also simply be read. Topics include: God's view of work, calling, success
and failure, time, money and stress, www.licc.org.uk.

For more materials on whole-life discipleship and work, including free resources and
downloads, go to www.licc.org.uk.

God at Work Course
The *God at Work* course aims to equip Christians to live out their Christian calling at
work and find purpose in every aspect of their working lives. The course provides a
Christian perspective on how to face challenges at work, as well as teaching on how to
support our family and friends in the difficulties we all inevitably face. The six sessions
cover: why work matters, ambition, tough decisions and choices, stress and work-life
balance; failure, disappointment and hope; money and mission. For more information
and all the resources you need to run the course visit http://godatwork.org.uk.

Alpha in the Workplace
This course provides a practical introduction to the Christian faith over 7 to 15
sessions. It is an opportunity for people of all backgrounds to explore the meaning
of life in a familiar and convenient location and is designed to fit into a regular
working day, e.g. over a lunch hour or run after work. There are courses running from
boardrooms to factories and from local coffee shops to those run through virtual
online networks. All the materials for running a course are online, downloadable and
easy to use. Find out more at http://alpha.org/workplace.

Working Every Day with Purpose

Ken Costa

Most people want to make a difference with their lives. To do this, we have to identify our part in extending God's kingdom and find out how we can bring blessing to the world. For many of us our part in extending God's kingdom takes place in the workplace, an environment which often leaves us unclear and confused about how God could value our daily activities and how our office space could possibly be seen as a mission opportunity. As an investment banker in the City of London, I have read the *Financial Times* and the Bible almost every day for the last 30 years. People often ask how I reconcile being a banker and a Christian. There is a widespread view that God and business simply don't mix: the competitive, cut-throat demands of the marketplace are seen as the obvious enemy of Christian compassion and love. But I have found that the God who created and sustains the world is also the God of the workplace. The world of work doesn't belong in the slipstream of twenty-first-century Christian spirituality, but in its mainstream. That's how God meant it to be. If the Christian faith is not relevant in the workplace, it is not relevant at all. Finding purpose in our work is one of the greatest challenges we face but taking the time to understand how God values our work, and how we can be a light for Christ in our work, enables us to view our day-to-day world very differently. All work has two main opportunities. The first is an opportunity to **worship** because our work stations are our worship stations. Worship is the total submission of our whole person to the glory of God as we recognise our dependence on him. Our workplaces should therefore be places of worship. Indeed, the Hebrew word for work and worship is the same – *avodah*. God is our real employer. Second, work is also a **witness** opportunity. It is important to remember that our primary purpose at work is to do the job that we are being paid to do. Yet, when we do this to the best of our ability and with the utmost Christian integrity, then opportunities for evangelism will probably follow. Every Christian can be a missionary in their workplace, and workplaces are often in just as much need of God as the far-flung countries that missionaries traditionally go to.

> The God who created and sustains the world is also God of the workplace.

The workplace is also where faith is tested and sharpened by day-to-day encounters with the ambiguities and stresses of modern commerce. Our faith is tested when we recognise our weaknesses at work and we learn more about our hard and soft spots in our working relationships precisely because we cannot always choose the people with whom we work. For the most part, I have had the privilege of hugely enjoying my work but there are moments when a sense of depression seems to hover over me at work. The causes are often deep-seated, but the triggers go off unexpectedly – a failed transaction, a disappointing pay review, unpleasant relationships, fear of the future. These times of trial happen to everyone. They are, however, opportunities for God to be glorified. Paul said, 'When I am weak, then I am strong' (2 Corinthians 12:10). I have come to see that weakness is very hard to show in the workplace unless we remember its object is strength – our dependence on God.

Over the past 20 years I have battled with many of the big questions often asked by Christians in the workplace and spent many an hour discussing these issues with trusted friends and members of my church at Holy Trinity Brompton. It was through these discussions I was encouraged to write the book *God at Work* which has since developed into a course. The course can be run in any church and uses six sessions to cover why work matters, the place of ambition, tough decisions and choices, stress and work-life balance, failure, disappointment and hope, and money and mission. For more details and information on how to get hold of the course materials see page 49.

The Light of Our Work

I am often struck by the fact that Jesus did not just say that he was the light of the world (John 8:12), but he told all his followers that we, too, are to be the light of the world, following his example:

> *You are the light of the world. A city on a hill cannot be hidden. Neither do people light a lamp and put it under a bowl. Instead they put it on its stand, and it gives light to everyone in the house. In the same way, let your light shine before men, that they may see your good deeds and glorify your Father in heaven* (Matthew 5:14–16).

You are the light of the world. A city on a hill cannot be hidden.

Jesus calls us to be radiant for him in our workplaces. We are to shine brightly for our Father in heaven with whoever or whatever comes into contact with us. Yet we can conceal the light in at least three ways.

The first way we can conceal the light is *physically*. The solution to this is **interaction**. The danger can be that, while we spend time in the workplace, we never truly rub shoulders with anyone. Sometimes we put our head down and do our work as fast as possible so that we can get out of work as early as possible, leaving little time for interaction with others. The reality is that interaction with our colleagues is a good, important and godly thing. As we begin to spend time with colleagues, particularly over lunch or after work, we can begin to share our lives with them and, with our lives, the gospel. Going to the pub with a colleague and chatting about the big questions of life is just as much a ministry as leading a course at church.

The second way that we can conceal the light is *morally*. When Jesus speaks of our light shining, he is primarily referring to our 'good deeds' (v.16). Yet so often we let the culture of our workplace transform us, when Christ longs to use us to transform our workplace and for us to be people of **integrity**. Of course, we will not live perfect lives at work and it is good to be honest and admit our failures and apologise to others when we are wrong. But we should aim, empowered by the Holy Spirit, to live and work with as much integrity as we can.

The third way we can conceal the light is *verbally*. If we never mention our connection to Jesus, then people will end up praising us, rather than 'praising our Father in heaven' (v.16). As the American pastor, John Piper, writes, 'Thinking that our work will glorify God when people do not know that we are Christians, is like admiring an effective ad on TV that never mentions the product. People may be impressed but they won't know what to buy.' One of the most natural things we can do is to **invite** our colleagues to 'come and see', just as Philip encouraged Nathanael to 'come and see' Jesus (John 1:46). This may be through our discussions or we might invite them to church or an event where they can hear about Jesus. For example, I once invited a colleague to come to an Alpha supper at my church. Amazingly he came, and I did little else but pray for him, but he became a Christian and he now heads up Alpha across all of Asia. At HTB we have increasingly realised that it is often easier to encourage others to 'come and see' Jesus whilst physically remaining in your workplace, rather than dragging them all the way to your Sunday church. That's why we have specifically tailored the Alpha course for the workplace, and many workplace Christian groups now run their own courses. The content is similar to the Alpha course but sessions are shorter so groups can meet before or after work, or during a lunch break. To find out more about Alpha in the Workplace and how to get hold of materials see page 49. It continues to excite me when I hear about the many ways people are using Alpha in the Workplace to share their faith. There are courses running from boardrooms to factories and from local coffee shops to those run through virtual online networks. I personally found running a course in my workplace to be a fun and rewarding experience and one I look forward to repeating in the near future.

Ken is the Chairman of Alpha International and author of God at Work.

> One of the most natural things we can do is to invite our colleagues to 'come and see'.

Stories of Witness in the Workplace

Mark Greene

God works through his people in a whole host of loving ways – to bless others, to bless the work and to communicate the gospel directly. Here are a few stories about God at work, through his people at work.

Passing strangers and the power of a smile

And it came to pass that in an ordinary, fairly large pharmaceutical company, a young scientist called Anita would, in the course of her work, walk down the office corridor. From time to time, a particular woman from another department would pass by and Anita would smile. Anita did not know her name and could only guess at her job. And the other woman, Gabriella, would smile in return. Occasionally, a little 'hello' would accompany the smile but they had no occasion to pause or chat, for both had work to do and places to go and people to meet whose names they knew. And besides, the work of the one did not touch the work of the other. And so time passed, counted in smiles and little 'hellos'.

And so it was that at the end of an ordinary day Anita was walking to her car and there, coming towards her, was Gabriella. They stopped and began to talk, Gabriella telling Anita that her four-year-old child was chronically ill with asthma and eczema that would not go away and that she wanted to leave her husband. Anita listened and asked if she could pray for her and if her home group could pray for her child. Gabriella said 'yes' and Anita offered her a Bible from the box of Bibles in the boot of her car.

The next day they met for lunch. And Anita prayed. And her home group prayed.

Within six months Gabriella's son was completely healed of his eczema and his asthma had subsided significantly. And Gabriella did not leave her husband but drew close to him and to Christ and to his people.

So Anita cared. Anita prayed. Anita shared the good news and was ready with materials to help Gabriella to get to know God. And Anita involved others in prayer.

Simple.

And by God's grace life-transforming.

Disarming response

'What do you think God's taught you at work that you've become good at?' the leader asked.

'Well,' Ian replied, 'I'm in the armed response unit and people in armed response tend to be pretty macho, tend to face-off with one another quite a bit, so there can be a lot of tension. Over the years I've found that I'm pretty good at bringing people back together. And that's really important because when you go into a life-and-death situation with guns it's vital that you completely trust the person next to you.'

What's Ian done? 'Blessed are the peacemakers, for they will be called sons of God,' Jesus says in Matthew 5:9. And beyond that Ian has shown his colleagues how to forgive one another, he's taught them the way of the King . . . and they've tasted that it's good.

The conscience of the company

People have been extremely open towards the gospel.

'When I left my previous job,' Ron began, 'someone said to me, "I'm sorry you are going; you've been the conscience of this company."'

Well, that would be impressive if the company were ten people, but Ron was talking about the second largest mining company in the world – with 35,000 employees.

Andrew says . . .

I have found that my faith as a Christian can be a bit of an enigma for my hospital colleagues; there doesn't seem to be a box to fit me into. I have conservative moral views, like the Muslims, but unlike the Muslims I will join in the hospital socials and have fun. I will drink but not get drunk and arrange my annual leave around church events, but won't seem to make a big deal of Christian holidays. I am 'religious' but seem very different to the typical hospital chaplain. This creates a great opportunity for conversation and I have found work colleagues to be some of the most open people I have come across.

Hospitals are very pluralistic; with Sikhs, Hindus, Muslims and atheists all working alongside each other. When I have taken genuine efforts to understand their worldview, asking lots of questions, people have been extremely open towards the gospel. My greatest joy came when my nominal Hindu friend from medical school became a Christian at my church last year. It had been nine years of friendship, with lots of socials and holidays together, that culminated in him saying that he knew Christianity was genuine because he saw it lived in people's lives.

Andrew is a doctor and a member of the Christian Medical Fellowship.

Gareth says . . .

I don't share Christ with everyone I meet and sometimes I can go months without telling anyone about him at all but I have found three tactics useful for opening up conversations:

- First, I wear a cross or fish. This can encourage believers, so that they often ask you to pray with them, and perhaps they will pray for you. It acts as a possible conversation starter.

- Second, I try to keep an eye on the locker of each of my patients. If the Gideon Bible has moved, I ask them about it and what did they read? Often this will start a conversation.

- Third, I try to ask if they have any religious beliefs when I take a social history. I used to cringe when I started doing this but people can happily answer 'C of E' or 'None' without embarrassment, while a Jehovah's Witness might be glad you asked. The next part is answering their questions and I would recommend a *Confident Christianity* or *Saline Solution* course for anyone who feels they need practice or more confidence.

Gareth is a doctor and a member of the Christian Medical Fellowship.

These two stories are reprinted with permission from Foundations – A Survival Guide for Junior Doctors *published by CMF. To find out more about* Confident Christianity *or* Saline Solution *courses visit www.cmf.org.uk.*

I try to keep an eye on the locker of each of my patients. If the Gideon Bible has moved, I ask them about it and what did they read? Often this will start a conversation.

GENEROSITY & STEWARDSHIP

The Bountiful Harvest

Celebrating generosity at harvest
Stewardship

Over the following pages are four weeks' worth of studies which can be used whenever works best for you, either in the lead up to or during harvest. You could even arrange a week-long celebration with these studies interspersed amongst a wider programme of harvest activities and events!

Each study takes a look at the diverse harvests celebrated in the Old and New Testaments, sowing new thoughts and reaping fresh insight from these traditional periods of celebration in the lives of God's people. Challenging questions and discussion prompts will guide each group to think about the richness of God's provision and how they can express this in their own thankfulness and generosity in their community.

The studies are based on a series of blogs written by Craig Borlase and Stewardship, www. stewardship. org.uk/blog.

These studies have been provided by Stewardship, an organisation passionate about inspiring and resourcing Christians to live and give generously. Practical tools include their online giving accounts: a safe, single place from which to organise all of one's personal charitable giving and which each year sees around £50 million distributed to churches, charities and individuals in full-time Christian ministry. Resources include small group studies, such as these, which have been prepared specifically in support of HOPE, along with a wide range of other materials for personal or church use.

To find out more visit www.stewardship.org.uk.

STUDY 1:
THE HARVEST PARADOX

Purpose

To reconnect with the importance of harvest; to discover how the harvest gatherings were a huge time of celebration and thanksgiving for God's people and their relevance to us today.

Introduction

Here comes harvest time: annual festival of tinned goods and small children struggling to make it all the way up to the front of church without dropping a 400g can of beans on their feet.

Really? Is that what harvest festival is about? Cleaning out the murkier corners of the kitchen cupboards? Not according to the Bible. The Old Testament is big on instructions, even dealing with the mechanics of farming and feeding. It turns out these instructions have something to say to us today as well.

Ice breaker

Spend some time thinking about harvest festivals and celebrations you have been to in the past. Your church or community may hold a harvest supper. These may have been more important in the past or if you were brought up living in the country. Compare your memories with what your church currently does.

Spend a few moments sharing your experiences with your group.

In the Old Testament God's people celebrated three different harvests.

Reflection and Bible reading

In Western Europe we have one harvest at the end of the summer and traditionally the whole community, including children, would help gather in the grain and produce, storing up supplies for the long winter. In the Old Testament God's people celebrated three different harvests, each of which is intrinsically linked to one of the three key religious festivals. There's Passover (barley), Pentecost (wheat) and the Feast of the Tabernacles (fruit), and they are loaded with meaning.

The barley harvest

Read Leviticus 23:9–14 Offering the Firstfruits

The LORD said to Moses, 'Speak to the Israelites and say to them: "When you enter the land I am going to give you and you reap its harvest, bring to the priest a sheaf of the first grain you harvest. He is to wave the sheaf before the LORD so that it will be accepted on your behalf; the priest is to wave it on the day after the Sabbath. On the day you wave the sheaf, you must sacrifice as a burnt offering to the LORD a lamb a year old without defect, together with its grain offering of two-tenths of an ephah of fine flour mixed with oil – an offering made to the LORD by fire, a pleasing aroma – and its drink offering of a quarter of a hin of wine. You must not eat any bread, or roasted or new grain, until the very day you bring this offering to your God. This is to be a lasting ordinance for the generations to come, wherever you live.

The harvest of barley was actually in the spring. The day that follows the Passover Sabbath which happens in the spring is known as the Feast of Firstfruits. Leviticus 23:10 reminds us how on this day the priest was to bring 'a sheaf of the first grain' that had been harvested. God loves it when we put him first. Think for a moment about the importance that *firsts* play in the Bible: making offerings of the firstfruits; the firstborn; 'No-one, however, may dedicate the firstborn of an animal, since the firstborn already belongs to the LORD; whether an ox or a sheep, it is the LORD's', Leviticus 27:26; even in Revelation, God is concerned with our first love.

This first harvest is meant to remind us where our priorities lie.

The wheat harvest

Read Leviticus 23:15–17,21 The Feast of Weeks

From the day after the Sabbath, the day you brought the sheaf of the wave offering, count off seven full weeks. Count off fifty days up to the day after the seventh Sabbath, and then present an offering of new grain to the LORD. From wherever you live, bring two loaves made of two-tenths of an ephah of fine flour, baked with yeast, as a wave offering of firstfruits to the LORD . . . On that same day you are to proclaim a sacred assembly and do no regular work. This is to be a lasting ordinance for the generations to come, wherever you live.

Some seven to eight weeks after the barley harvest comes the time for wheat to be gathered. The wheat harvest was celebrated through the Feast of Weeks (sometimes known as the Feast of Harvest), and it was a Jewish holy day. That's why the disciples were gathered in the Upper Room in Jerusalem – observing religious custom – when the Holy Spirit showed up and Pentecost kicked off.

The Feast of Weeks was celebrated by people bringing an offering of bread made from the first wheat harvest: the new grain mentioned in Leviticus. They were reminded of the transforming power of God, of his provision, his harvest. Pentecost extends this theme, bringing to mind the great harvest of 3,000 souls on that one day, as well as the power of God's Spirit to transform us.

The fruit harvest

Read Leviticus 23:33–44 The Feast of Tabernacles

The LORD said to Moses, 'Say to the Israelites: "On the fifteenth day of the seventh month the LORD's Feast of Tabernacles begins, and it lasts for seven days. The first day is a sacred assembly; do no regular work. For seven days present offerings made to the LORD by fire, and on the eighth day hold a sacred assembly and present an offering made to the LORD by fire. It is the closing assembly; do no regular work.

('"These are the LORD's appointed feasts, which you are to proclaim as sacred assemblies for bringing offerings made to the LORD by fire – the burnt offerings and grain offerings, sacrifices and drink offerings required for each day. These offerings are in addition to those for the LORD's Sabbaths and in addition to your gifts and whatever you have vowed and all the freewill offerings you give to the LORD.)

'"So beginning with the fifteenth day of the seventh month, after you have gathered the crops of the land, celebrate the festival to the LORD for seven days; the first day is a day of rest, and the eighth day also is a day of rest. On the first day you are to take branches from the trees, and palm fronds, leafy branches and poplars, and rejoice before the LORD your God for seven days. Celebrate this as a festival to the LORD for seven days each year. This is to be a lasting ordinance for the generations to come; celebrate it in the seventh month. Live in booths for seven days: All native-born Israelites are to live in booths so that your descendants will know that I made the Israelites live in booths when I brought them out of Egypt. I am the LORD your God.'"

So Moses announced to the Israelites the appointed feasts of the LORD.

What can we do to remember to be thankful always?

The fruit harvest is called the Feast of Tabernacles, and brought to mind the bounty, provision and protection of God. The celebration lasted a week and even today those observing the Feast will spend the time living in temporary, fragile shelters – as instructed in Leviticus 23:39–43. Also known as Sukkot, the joy that was experienced as people harvested the fruit from the trees meant that this harvest was known as the 'season of joy'. The Feast of Tabernacles was a time of great celebration, knowing that your sins had been forgiven and of God's miraculous provision.

Questions for discussion

- In the Old Testament, harvest celebrations happened three times a year. They were always a celebration of thankfulness for God's provision. What can we do to remember to be thankful always?

- The wheat harvest, the Feast of Weeks, involved people bringing an offering of bread. Consider the effort required to grind, make and bake that bread; the effort to go and get firewood. Now consider what effort we use to bring our harvest offering. Should we change what we do?

- The harvest celebration was always about giving the first crop or the best to God first. If you were given some money, would you consider giving some or all of it away? Explain your answers.
- In what other practical ways could you 'give God the best'? Think through your time, skills, serving others and practising hospitality. Do you give your 'best'?

Conclusion and prayer

The tin cans we shove into plastic bags at harvest are a poor symbol of God's abundance and generosity. This year let's reconnect with the idea of celebrating our God who protects, provides and who never leaves us.

Begin your prayer time offering thanks and praise to God:

- For how he has provided for you (recently).
- For how he has protected you and your family.
- For the promises he has yet to fulfil over you.

Spend time praying about how you can give the firstfruits, and how you can contribute your 'best'.

The harvest celebration was always about giving the first crop or the best to God first. If you were given some money, would you consider giving some or all of it away?

STUDY 2:
HARVEST AND JUSTICE

Purpose

To discover how God set down rules for providing for the poor and marginalised in Old Testament societies and how his provision for the less well-off should challenge us in our own community roles today.

Introduction

Chances are you're familiar with the biblical story of Ruth already, but does the book leap to mind when the harvest festival wall displays go up at school? Probably not! But Ruth's story has plenty to offer and is well worth a read today.

Ice breaker

Look up the meaning of your name – have you 'grown into it'? Does it ring true to your character?

(To save time, the leader may want to look up the names of those in the group beforehand.)

Don't worry if your name doesn't seem to mean anything profound! In the Bible, God was in the business of giving people new names and he can give you another one to grow into:

Abram ('high father') became Abraham ('father of a multitude') Genesis 17:5

Sarai ('my princess') became Sarah ('mother of nations') Genesis 17:15

Jacob ('supplanter') became Israel ('having power with God') Genesis 32:28

Simon ('God has heard') became Peter ('rock') John 1:42

> Look up the meaning of your name – have you 'grown into it'?

Reflection and Bible reading

At the beginning of the book of Ruth we are introduced to the plight of Naomi and her family. Naomi is hit by the deaths of her husband and two sons, left in a foreign town with no option other than to release her daughters-in-law to go back home. Yet Ruth chooses not to abandon her grieving mother-in-law (Ruth 1:16–18). Even though the law allows her to leave, Ruth chooses to stay. Legalism has its limits: sometimes we need to abandon the principle of giving 'just enough' or helping 'in our own little way' and offer the best of what we have – our time, our energy, our potential.

Chapter 2 sees Naomi and Ruth arrive back in Naomi's home town. No longer travellers, able to rely on the hospitality of others, they must find their own food and fight for their own survival. But God has a plan – a law – that comes to their rescue. The practice of 'gleaning' – the principle of not picking up the harvest leftovers from the ground and not reaping right to the very corners of the field – is described in Leviticus 23:22, and it comes to Ruth and Naomi's rescue. Maybe legalism does have its place after all.

Read Ruth Chapter 2

Now Naomi had a relative on her husband's side from the clan of Elimelech, a man of standing, whose name was Boaz.

And Ruth the Moabitess said to Naomi, 'Let me go to the fields and pick up the leftover grain behind anyone in whose eyes I find favour.'

Naomi said to her, 'Go ahead, my daughter.' So she went out and began to glean in the fields behind the harvesters. As it turned out, she found herself working in a field belonging to Boaz, who was from the clan of Elimelech.

Just then Boaz arrived from Bethlehem and greeted the harvesters, 'The LORD be with you!'

'May you be richly rewarded by the LORD.'

'The LORD bless you!' they called back.

Boaz asked the foreman of his harvesters, 'Whose young woman is that?'

The foreman replied, 'She is the Moabitess who came back from Moab with Naomi. She said, "Please let me glean and gather among the sheaves behind the harvesters." She went into the field and has worked steadily from morning till now, except for a short rest in the shelter.'

So Boaz said to Ruth, 'My daughter, listen to me. Don't go and glean in another field and don't go away from here. Stay here with my servant girls. Watch the field where the men are harvesting, and follow along after the girls. I have told the men not to touch you. And whenever you are thirsty, go and get a drink from the water jars the men have filled.'

At this, she bowed down with her face to the ground. She exclaimed, 'Why have I found such favour in your eyes that you notice me – a foreigner?'

Boaz replied, 'I've been told all about what you have done for your mother-in-law since the death of your husband – how you left your father and mother and your homeland and came to live with a people you did not know before. May the LORD repay you for what you have done. May you be richly rewarded by the LORD, the God of Israel, under whose wings you have come to take refuge.'

'May I continue to find favour in your eyes, my lord,' she said. 'You have given me comfort and have spoken kindly to your servant – though I do not have the standing of one of your servant girls.'

At mealtime Boaz said to her, 'Come over here. Have some bread and dip it in the wine vinegar.'

When she sat down with the harvesters, he offered her some roasted grain. She ate all she wanted and had some left over. As she got up to glean, Boaz gave orders to his men, 'Even if she gathers among the sheaves, don't embarrass her. Rather, pull out some stalks for her from the bundles and leave them for her to pick up, and don't rebuke her.'

So Ruth gleaned in the field until evening. Then she threshed the barley she had gathered, and it amounted to about an ephah. She carried it back to town, and her mother-in-law saw how much she had gathered. Ruth also brought out and gave her what she had left over after she had eaten enough.

Her mother-in-law asked her, 'Where did you glean today? Where did you work? Blessed be the man who took notice of you!'

Then Ruth told her mother-in-law about the one at whose place she had been working. 'The name of the man I worked with today is Boaz,' she said.

'The LORD bless him!' Naomi said to her daughter-in-law. 'He has not stopped showing his kindness to the living and the dead.' She added, 'That man is our close relative; he is one of our kinsman-redeemers.'

Then Ruth the Moabitess said, 'He even said to me, "Stay with my workers until they finish harvesting all my grain."'

Naomi said to Ruth her daughter-in-law, 'It will be good for you, my daughter, to go with his girls, because in someone else's field you might be harmed.'

So Ruth stayed close to the servant girls of Boaz to glean until the barley and wheat harvests were finished. And she lived with her mother-in-law.

'Where did you glean today? Where did you work?'

Questions for discussion

Read Leviticus 19:9–10 and Deuteronomy 24:19

Discuss anything that stands out. In today's individualistic society, how do these passages challenge or inspire you?

Read Leviticus 19:9–10

When you reap the harvest of your land, do not reap to the very edges of your field or gather the gleanings of your harvest. Do not go over your vineyard a second time or pick up the grapes that have fallen. Leave them for the poor and the alien. I am the LORD your God.

Are there any traits in Boaz that you would particularly aspire to?

Read Deuteronomy 24:19

When you are harvesting in your field and you overlook a sheaf, do not go back to get it. Leave it for the alien, the fatherless and the widow, so that the LORD your God may bless you in all the work of your hands.

Re-read Ruth 2:4,8–9,14,16

Just then Boaz arrived from Bethlehem and greeted the harvesters, 'The LORD be with you!' . . . So Boaz said to Ruth, 'My daughter, listen to me. Don't go and glean in another field and don't go away from here. Stay here with my servant girls. Watch the field where the men are harvesting, and follow along after the girls. I have told the men not to touch you. And whenever you are thirsty, go and get a drink from the water jars the men have filled' . . . At mealtime Boaz said to her, 'Come over here. Have some bread and dip it in the wine vinegar' . . . 'Rather, pull out some stalks for her from the bundles and leave them for her to pick up, and don't rebuke her.'

* What kind of man was Boaz?
* Do you know anyone else like him?
* Are there any traits in Boaz that you would particularly aspire to?
* Do you think Boaz would have treated Ruth in the same way if it weren't for the family connection? Discuss.

Re-read Ruth 2: 6–7

The foreman replied, 'She is the Moabitess who came back from Moab with Naomi. She said, "Please let me glean and gather among the sheaves behind the harvesters." She went into the field and has worked steadily from morning till now, except for a short rest in the shelter.'

It was Boaz's workers who originally let Ruth work in the field. They obviously knew their master's convictions about following the law and ministering to the poor and the foreigner. How does this challenge you when thinking about your relationship with God?

Conclusion

The name Boaz means 'a pillar of society' (also the name given to one of the pillars in the temple incidentally) and Ruth's name means 'friend'. Is there a connection between a name and who someone becomes or is it a coincidence that occurs when God's laws for justice are obeyed?

Prayer

- As part of your prayer time, thank God that he is a God of justice and he has a heart for the oppressed.
- Invite the group to mention individuals and communities that are on the edge of society.
- Look into your own hearts and think about the contributions you make or could make.
- Pray that you may be aware of anything that God is asking or challenging you to do.

As part of your prayer time, thank God that he is a God of justice and he has a heart for the oppressed.

STUDY 3:
PLANNING FOR THE HARVEST

Purpose

To reclaim the importance of the cycle of reaping and sowing, seedtime and harvest and to look at what are the priorities when it comes to planning for the future and where we sow our seeds.

Introduction

As long as the earth endures, seedtime and harvest, cold and heat, summer and winter, day and night will never cease.

In Genesis 8:22, God says there will be seedtime and harvest as long as the earth remains. These words were spoken to Noah as he looked at the earth completely destroyed by the flood. In other words, God was letting him know he could start over with the seeds in his hand.

Just as in Noah's time any modern-day farmer knows the key to a successful crop is all in the planning. Even then, with the best tools and years of experience, it can be a hazardous task: deciding which seed stock to plant, fertilisers, equipment, weed control and negotiating the vagaries of the weather systems.

Ice breaker

Think about the plans you have made in the past or are thinking about making. Some plans are life-changing such as getting married or planning for retirement. Other plans can be around learning a new skill for your career or planning a training programme for running a marathon. Other plans are more trivial: next year's holiday, organising a fundraising event or a family celebration.

Think about plans you have made this year and share some big and some smaller plans with the rest of the group.

Write on a big piece of paper all the different types of plans we make.

Planning is the big picture, but the harvest abundance that is reaped is reliant on the seeds sown.

Reflection and Bible reading

Read 2 Corinthians 9:6–12

Remember this: Whoever sows sparingly will also reap sparingly, and whoever sows generously will also reap generously. Each man should give what he has decided in his heart to give, not reluctantly or under compulsion, for God loves a cheerful giver. And God is able to make all grace abound to you, so that in all things at all times, having all that you need, you will abound in every good work. As it is written: 'He has scattered abroad his gifts to the poor; his righteousness endures for ever.' Now he who supplies seed to the sower and bread for food will also supply and increase your store of seed and will enlarge the harvest of your righteousness. You will be made rich in every way so that you can be generous on every occasion, and through us your generosity will result in thanksgiving to God. This service that you perform is not only supplying the needs of God's people but is also overflowing in many expressions of thanks to God.

We come face to face with some bumper sticker verses here: 'Whoever sows generously will also reap generously' (v.6), 'God loves a cheerful giver' (v.7) and 'God is able to make all grace abound to you' (v.8). If you weren't a fan of context you could take these as fuel to fire a prosperity gospel. Sadly, that's not quite what Paul has in mind, but the passage is still dynamite when it comes to the subject of our giving.

> Each of us should give 'what he has decided in his heart to give'.

Paul's right when he says that we reap what we sow, but we should remember that Paul is using the agricultural term metaphorically here, and so we are not meant to take the words literally. Instead of giving as a transaction, Paul paints a picture of a bolder, brighter way of being, one where our choices are motivated by our heart rather than our wallet. Each of us should give 'what he has decided in his heart to give'. As the late John Stott commented, 'There is a sense here of a settled conviction about how much to give; of a decision reached after careful consideration, and always with joy and cheerfulness.'

Stott also made the link between this passage and Paul's earlier letter to the Corinthians where he encourages planned, systematic giving (1 Corinthians 16:1–3). While there's nothing wrong with spontaneous Spirit-prompted acts of generosity, we primarily need to approach the matter with care, prayer and time. Decisions about what, and how, we give should not be left to spur-of-the-moment emotions, just as harvest cannot be reaped without preparations or a holiday plan itself.

Questions for discussion

- Do you take stock and plan your giving in terms of time, talents, skills and income? In light of this passage do you think it is important?
- These verses in Corinthians have been misinterpreted in the past. Taken in context, what does verse 9 mean to you? Reading on to verse 10 may help.

As it is written: 'He has scattered abroad his gifts to the poor; his righteousness endures for ever.' Now he who supplies seed to the sower and bread for food will also supply and increase your store of seed and will enlarge the harvest of your righteousness.

- Verse 6 reminds us that if we sow sparingly we will reap sparingly but if we sow generously, we will reap generously. In the parable of the sower in Mark 4, Jesus talks about sowing the word of God in the soil of our hearts. Where and how can we sow and plant good seeds?

- The seed of the word can easily be smothered by the 'worries of this life, the deceitfulness of wealth and the desires for other things'. What steps do we need to take to halt this smothering process?

- The farmer has to wait for the harvest; we sow in one season and reap in another. Are we good at investing our efforts in things where there is no quick gain or return? Are we patient enough like the farmer to wait and watch?

Conclusion

Harvests, like generosity, take time, purposeful planning and an eye for the long game. As well as making us more efficient in our giving, this also allows for a greater connection with God through the process. As Paul says: *'This service that you perform is not only supplying the needs of God's people but is also overflowing in many expressions of thanks to God'* (2 Corinthians 9:12).

Prayer

'If you want to make God laugh, tell him your plans.'

Woody Allen is credited with saying, 'If you want to make God laugh, tell him your plans.' His apt remark reminds us that we need to humbly come before God with our plans, visions and ideas.

- Spend some time praying about the plans you have as individuals and as a group.

- Pray about some of the challenges we face when planting seeds.

- Giving doesn't just happen! We are motivated to give by many things: love, guilt, gratitude, favouritism or justice. Spend some time in quiet meditation reflecting on your giving.

Giving doesn't just happen! We are motivated to give by many things: love, guilt, gratitude, favouritism or justice.

STUDY 4:
THE GLOBAL HARVEST –
AUSTERITY vs ABUNDANCE

Purpose

To reconnect with the seasons and the importance of harvest time and God's provision; to think about the global harvest and where and how our food is grown and how we can be responsible consumers.

Introduction

Faith has plenty to say about finance and friendship, but should it have any bearing on our food?

According to Martin Luther King the answer is 'yes'. He said: 'Before you finish eating your breakfast this morning, you've depended on half the world. This is the way our universe is structured . . . we aren't going to have peace on earth until we recognise this basic fact.'

Even back in the 1960s Martin Luther King understood that modern life goes hand in hand with globalisation.

Ice breaker

In which month are the following fruits and vegetables at their best (in season)?

Cox apples
Broad beans
Asparagus
Blackberries
Brussels sprouts
Spring green cabbage
Red cabbage
Carrots
Cauliflower
Cherries
Leeks
Cos lettuce

Answers: Cox apples (October); broad beans (June); asparagus (May); blackberries (September); Brussels sprouts (December); spring green cabbage (March); red cabbage (November); carrots (January); cauliflower (April); cherries (July); leeks (February); Cos lettuce (August)

Reflection and Bible reading

We might like to think that our tomatoes have been grown with care. It's far more likely that they were harvested while still under-ripe by poorly waged women in the developing world, before being shipped or flown in gas-tight containers while mysterious chemicals helped ripen them to cosmetic perfection along their journey to the vacuum-packed West.

But while our food connects us with distant communities we've never heard of, many of us are left feeling more *disconnected* from food than ever.

Disconnected? Yes. There are no seasons within supermarkets: strawberries and salad could just as easily be served at Christmas as they could in summer. The link between lunch and land, calories and climate, food and farmer, have been all but lost to us. These days there are few of us who have sheaves of barley or wheat, or even bulging stores of fruit that we have gathered in the fading autumn sun, and it's paradoxical that we still celebrate a festival that is so removed from our common experience.

Read Ecclesiastes 3:1–8

There is a time for everything,
and a season for every activity under heaven:
a time to be born and a time to die,
a time to plant and a time to uproot,
a time to kill and a time to heal,
a time to tear down and a time to build,
a time to weep and a time to laugh,
a time to mourn and a time to dance,
a time to scatter stones and a time to gather them,
a time to embrace and a time to refrain,
a time to search and a time to give up,
a time to keep and a time to throw away,
a time to tear and a time to mend,
a time to be silent and a time to speak,
a time to love and a time to hate,
a time for war and a time for peace.

Questions for discussion

- Seasons were incredibly important in the lives of Bible characters. Without the infrastructure available to us now, and without chemicals and preservatives, the nation of Israel relied upon good harvests and seasonal foods. Life was far more defined by seasons. Was this a good thing? Discuss.

- Food isn't the only major life theme which has seasons. Have a look at the Ecclesiastes passage and identify two or three of the seasons mentioned which you can relate to.

- A number of the 'a time to . . .' phrases are linked in some way to community. Do you think that the development of a global community has helped or hindered our experience of these issues in the context of our immediate community? For example, are we more or less able to weep and laugh together, etc.?

- The idea of seasons implies a time of waiting for something. Think of something that you have to wait for in life, and some things that you previously had to wait for (when you were younger) and discuss the positives and negatives of waiting for things (rather than receiving everything instantly).

> The idea of seasons implies a time of waiting for something.

Conclusion

We do have something in common with the generations that have gone before us: the opportunity to take time to deliberately remind ourselves of all that God has provided, to celebrate this created world and revel in the sustaining beauty of food.

Prayer

(The leader may wish to have researched the source of some global foods and how they are grown and harvested.)

- Reflect on the season of autumn. Spend some time thinking about this month (colours, leaves, shorter days, cooler mornings, birds having flown, etc.).

- Think about where some of your favourite food comes from – coffee, chocolate, fruit, rice – and pray for the seasonal workers, farmers, producers, etc.

- Pick out a couple of verses from the passage that speak to you at the moment and spend some time meditating on them.

For more harvest resources, including special videos you can download, head to the Stewardship website, www.stewardship.org.uk/harvest.

Thankfulness, Generosity and Mission

Tearfund

Whenever we consider the nature of God, we cannot get far without encountering a powerful reminder of God's incredible generosity. From the dawn of creation, through centuries spent nurturing his chosen people, right up to the birth and death and resurrection of his only Son, we are reminded that God's nature is pure generosity.

We are reminded that God's nature is pure generosity. Just as John 3:16 reminds us that 'God so loved the world that he gave . . .' in the rest of scripture we find plenty of reminders of the driving force behind human generosity. And what better illustration than Jesus' encounter with the 'sinful woman'? Her act of lavish generosity was caused by love – a direct response to the knowledge that her sins had been forgiven. Jesus himself underlines the truth, stating that when we become aware of the power of God's love to cleanse us, we cannot help but feel full to overflowing with gratitude.

This remains relevant for us today. Christ's feet may have stopped leaving fresh prints on our soil – and our backgrounds may be different – but haven't we all been rescued by the loving forgiveness of God? Don't we all have reason to weep at his feet in gratitude for what he has done for us?

The answer is 'yes'. But to whom should we show that gratitude? Towards the end of his ministry Jesus declared that 'whatever you did for one of the least of these brothers of mine, you did for me' (Matthew 25:40), making it clear that the search for opportunities to express our gratitude to God should be conducted with eyes wide open out beyond the walls of the church.

James is beautifully direct when tackling this subject. It's no use our making grand statements if our faith and love are inert. If we want to show gratitude to God there's no better place to start than among those on the margins of our society.

This theme of being motivated to reach out beyond ourselves by Christ's love for us is echoed in the parable of the Good Samaritan (Luke 10:25ff). The story has been drilled into those of us who grew up in Sunday school, yet the lessons it offers can take a lifetime to absorb. Who is the good neighbour, we are asked? The outcast, we reply, the one despised by those with status and power. The parable beautifully reminds us that in seeking to uphold the first commandment to love God with all our heart, soul and strength we must not forget the second: to love our neighbours as ourselves. These 'neighbours' are not defined by clan, creed or country. Instead they are simply those who are in need of our help. Where there is need, there are neighbours. Do we have the vision to see them?

Be Thankful for Where You Are

It might not be the first thing that springs to mind, but being thankful for where we live is an important attitude for churches to adopt. In spite of the headlines and falling red lines on statisticians' graphs, churches still have incredible potential when it comes to local communities. And, like the little boy who gave up his lunch of fish and bread, our decision to respond in generosity to those around us can so easily be multiplied by our Lord God.

In 2008, ICM were commissioned to carry out some research to find out how much people on the same street interact with each other. Amongst other things, the survey discovered:

- More than a fifth (22%) of Britons believe that the UK's neighbourhoods have become less friendly in the last five years.

- Half of Britons said hello to fewer than six people in their street during the previous week – *and one in ten of those questioned had spoken to no one.*

- Some now think there is a serious decline in everyday interaction – *and argue that this leads to needless disputes.*

- 36% of us would not trust anybody who lived in our street with our keys – *among 25- to 34-year-olds this figure is almost half.*

Half of Britons said hello to fewer than six people in their street during the previous week.

With that in mind, here are a few ideas which might help your church connect in new ways with what it means to be good neighbours and to be thankful for where God has placed us.

Photo collage

Get together in groups – with friends, neighbours and people from church – and take some cameras out and about in your community. Take photos of the good things you see and the positive changes that have been made. Come back together and create a positive community collage.

Hit the press

Gather all your local papers and cut out any pieces that you think show actions that are worth celebrating. Compile all your cuttings into a collage and display it in – or outside – your church.

Monthly dinners

If you are able to, you could invite a new neighbour to dinner each month, starting with a harvest meal.

Celebrate your community

Get out and ask people in your community what they love about where they live and what could make life in your area even better. You might be surprised by what you hear. Find ways to share your results so that everyone can see the positives.

Use the information on page 75 to take things a step further and really get to know your community so you know how best to approach mission activities.

And Finally, Pray . . .

A Liturgical Prayer

Our Father, who brings heaven to earth,
Merciful and mighty Son who guards our hearts,
Compassionate and counselling Spirit who walks with us,
We stand in prayer with our Christian brothers and sisters around the world,
In places where food is scarce and hunger powerful.
And with them we pray for your light to burn brightly on their work.
As we pour out our prayers, pour out your mercy to answer us.

Merciful and mighty Son, Sender of good gifts, bringer of life, worker of miracles,
You have given your church your own heart.
Help us, through our prayers and actions, to enable local churches to lift the broken,
To release the potential which resides in even the poorest communities,
As we pour out our prayers, pour out your mercy to answer us.

Compassionate and counselling Spirit,
We commit ourselves, as part of your global church movement,
To play our part in bringing a kingdom of justice,
In bringing spiritual and material transformation into the darkest places,
In being part of the church – and releasing its potential to be your agent of change in the poorest of places.
As we pour out our prayers, pour out your mercy to answer us.

We pray for strength to fulfil your call to us, to care for the orphan, to feed the hungry,
To release the potential of poor communities so that they may find a better future.
Hear us, your servants.
Amen.

Prayer idea for small groups

Choose an evening and ask everyone to bring two or three favourite scriptures from the Bible on giving thanks. Next, start to ask everyone to make a list of the many things we receive from God, covering all the spiritual, physical, emotional, intellectual, material and relational blessings he gives. Share some of those with each other then have a time of prayer inviting everyone to share short prayers of thanksgiving: 'Lord, I thank you for . . .' and see how long you can keep going! Encourage everyone to have a thanksgiving week where they take time every day to thank God for all that he gives. Then when the group next meets, take time to share and pray into all that has been learnt.

Get to Know Your Community

We might have some brilliant ideas about how we'd like to be generous to our communities this harvest, but to build up some great relationships and make good use of our gifts it's important to first find out what it is that our neighbours actually need and to work with them to achieve it.

Here are some ideas . . .

- Start by drawing a large map of your community. Plot out the church, the housing estates, shops, community buildings, roads and so on. Then add to it the areas where you sense there is poverty and social issues (from bored young people to substance misuse, homelessness and isolation). Show your map to a wider group within your church – do they agree? What's missing? Where are the neediest areas? Who are the most vulnerable groups? Do your neighbours and friends outside of church agree?

> Take time every day to thank God for all that he gives.

- You could hold a harvest fair or supper or use your harvest service to begin to engage the thoughts and ideas of the wider community. Set up a stall and lay out pieces of paper (or postcards) with various social issues written or illustrated on them – like debt, housing, health care, unemployment, crime, education. Invite people who pass by the table to vote on which issue is the most relevant. Give them five counters and ask them to 'spend' the counters where they think there is most need in the community by placing them onto the relevant postcards. At the end of the event you should have a good picture of what a sample of the community feel are priority issues of need.

- Talk to key contacts in your community, such as doctors, community police officers, social workers, other churches, child care services and others who might have an opinion. Ask them what they think are the key issues in the community, who are the main service providers addressing these issues and what are the gaps.

- Look at the statistics for your local area. Try entering your postcode into www.neighbourhood.statistics.gov.uk or www.upmystreet.com. What does it say about public service provision in your area? What do you learn about crime, local schools, health and employment?

- Design a questionnaire and carry out a community survey. You can post this out, but you are likely to get a better response if you do this face to face, plus it allows you to start building relationships with those outside of your church. This might involve knocking on doors, so make sure you prepare yourselves properly: when is an appropriate time to door knock? Explain why you are there, and how many questions you have! Have a good balance between closed questions (yes or no answers) and open questions.

Understand that our aim is to work with communities, not just for them.

- Organise a focus group meeting. This involves gathering a sample of the community together in one place and chairing a discussion about needs in the community. To encourage people to come you might want to provide food and drinks. Also, make sure you keep to time and ensure that participants understand the purpose of the meeting and how you plan to use the information afterwards. Make sure someone is taking notes on the discussion and that key points are recorded. An alternative to this would be to go out and visit other community groups, such as lunch clubs for the elderly, mum and toddler groups, youth clubs, etc. and ask the organisers if you can conduct your focus group at their meeting.

- Put on a regular community meal or coffee morning. These are often great ways to get to know your community and also provide a great service for people. Once they begin to feel more comfortable with you and you have built up a good relationship you can begin to ask them about the wider needs they see in the community. What else can the church do to help them and their neighbours?

Finally, once you have conducted this period of research and relationship building, you should have a clear sense of what your community needs – as well as who you can partner with to deliver it. To go into more depth we would recommend the *Inside Out* course and Discovery process. Visit www.communitymission.org.uk/courses for these and further resources.

Remember, Christianity was never meant to be a solo discipline: we were made to be connected, not only with our heavenly Father, but with our fellow humans. We were made for community, just as church was made to be a source of strength, support and hope for those living around it. To that end it's vital that as we consider ways in which we can connect with the world beyond the doors of the church, we understand that our aim is to work *with* communities, not just *for* them.

Generosity

Dr Rachel Jordan

Generosity usually means giving, and often we're quite comfortable with that, but it is equally important to be a generous receiver which is where we can often struggle. Do we ask for help from our friends and neighbours, from those who we're ministering amongst, the vulnerable? When they offer their help or their gifts do we know how to be generous receivers and bless their giving and generosity? Will we eat the food that someone else has made that might not be quite what we're used to or accept the gift, however small, because the giver needs the blessing of giving? We need to learn the reciprocal gift of generous, vulnerable receiving.

There is a strange power balance in giving and receiving and when we receive we are often making ourselves less powerful, being open to someone else's culture or style. We empower others when we receive their gifts, when we welcome what they offer to us. To do so without critique, without thinking that we could have given something better.

The widow in the Bible who gave her mite is a perfect picture of a generous giver who could have been overlooked. Jesus knew the value or her small offering, she gave from her poverty, her tiny monetary gift was an act of extreme generosity. Let us not miss those whose gifts look small but whose generosity is great. Let us give all people the opportunity to give and think before we judge the giver by the gift.

There is a strange power balance in giving and receiving.

I have the great privilege of being friends with some women who are, or have been, homeless and now attend a day centre in a women's hostel. One of these ladies has a roof over her head but has lost her benefits and has had no income for a year. She has been kept alive by the lady who runs the local café who has given her all the day-old sandwiches. The lady from the hostel was saying to me that she hoped the women's hostel (where we meet) would give out presents this year because she will then be able to give away the gift she receives to the lady in the café. What an extremely generous gift that will be. And when the lady in the café receives it, she will give back some dignity to the vulnerable woman.

So be generous, be vulnerable, and allow others the power to know that you need them and appreciate them.

Rachel is the National Adviser for Mission and Evangelism for the Church of England.

A Cycle of Generosity

Beth Milburn

Imagine you're waiting at a bus stop on a cold day. It's raining and you're getting soaked but then someone from your church pulls up and offers you a lift. This simple act has many different positive effects. You're likely to feel relief and gratitude, which are both powerful emotions, and the experience of being blessed by someone else's kindness makes you more likely to look for a good deed you can do that would help someone else. So a continually expanding chain begins with generosity spurring gratitude which spurs further generosity to others and so on. This isn't just positive because more people get helped out, but because it generates community which is what the church is all about. Generous acts help us to remove ourselves from the mind-set of a society filled with individualism, where thought processes and actions are orientated around 'looking after number one'. Generosity is a statement that says your life is not so busy or difficult that you cannot understand the needs of others and act on them out of love. This counter-cultural statement is what we should be striving for as Christians.

Imagine yourself in someone else's shoes.

Of course generosity must extend far beyond the church and I believe the best motivator for generosity is empathy. This involves imagination. Sympathy does stir generosity to a certain extent but an understanding of someone's situation does so much more. If you imagine yourself in someone else's shoes, mentally clothing yourself in their experiences, you will find it generates both the knowledge of what practical steps would help to relieve that person's load, and a more freely flowing, natural form of generosity which stems from the understanding that empathy creates.

Beth is 17 and lives in North Devon where she is finishing off her A levels before studying Politics and International Development at university.

Why Mission?

Tearfund

Ask people on the street which Christian has been the best ambassador for the faith and you'll most likely end up hearing names like William Wilberforce, Martin Luther King, Mother Teresa and Desmond Tutu. Why? Because each of them has been defined by a Christian faith that has found expression through the power and courage of their actions. These are the people who applied their faith to more than the Sunday service. They took their beliefs out to the offices, the slums, the halls of power and the prison cells. Each endured injustice and hardship and made a real, concrete difference to the world. Little wonder, therefore, that their lives speak of God's love more powerfully than any doctrine or creed.

Their lives speak of God's love more powerfully than any doctrine or creed.

Today we call such approaches 'integral mission', and they can be found driving local churches as they transform lives and communities across the world. Integral mission is fundamentally about how faith in Jesus Christ is embodied in all aspects of life – and how it makes a difference to the way we act in the real world.

Of course, the message of the gospel should change us. Repentance and forgiveness should never be taken lightly, but nor should they be seen as the final destination. In the Bible, inward beliefs can never be divorced from outward application – loving God has always meant loving your neighbour. And it always will.

Remember how Isaiah, Jeremiah, Micah and Amos denounced slick religious activity that ignored the injustices of the day? Remember how the teachings of John the Baptist, Jesus, Paul and John all resonate with the metaphor of the importance of our lives producing 'fruit'?

'Wisdom is proved right by her actions,' said Jesus (Matthew 11:19), and yet as evangelicals we have been guilty of scaling back the importance of our tangible, physical, practical expressions of faith. Jim Wallis has written:

> 'The churches have individualised the kingdom by restricting it to inner recesses of the heart; they have spiritualised it by removing it entirely to heaven; or they have futurised it by speaking of it only in connection to apocalyptic events at the end of time.'
>
> (Jim Wallis, *Agenda for Biblical People*, Harper and Row, 1984)

Finding ways to avoid this state is not so hard after all. What can be difficult is making the choice to take those first steps away from an inward-focused, other-worldly version of Christianity.

You can work together to support issues of injustice and global poverty.

At our best the church is a magnificent, life-changing body of people. We can break injustice, challenge oppression, offer hope to those left behind and bring the love of God into clear focus for people who never believed themselves worthy. But to do even a fraction of this we must go. We must turn away from the shallow waters of personal preference and religious ritual and venture deeper into the risky places where courage and conviction are vital. We must go – led by the Spirit and reliant on God for every step of the journey.

Will souls be saved? We believe it – though we know, too, that salvation is God's gift to us. What we do know for sure is that as our faith propels out, as our actions serve those in need, caring for them spiritually as well as materially, this world will see the revolution of hope take more and more ground.

Be Generous With Your Community This Harvest

We worship a God of justice who loves to see his children stand up for issues of justice and poverty. Why not help your community to be part of God's restoration of the world this harvest time? You can work together to support issues of injustice and global poverty – and in doing so is a great opportunity to get to know your community and to be able to build up the relationships that allow you to share your faith.

Why Not Walk in Their Shoes?

Elizabeth comes from Ogongora village in Uganda and has faced so many struggles. Childlessness left her ostracised by other members of her community, and an attack on her village by the brutal militia known as the Lord's Resistance Army (LRA) left her widowed, beaten and homeless. Like so many others, Elizabeth had no option other than to flee her village and join other survivors in an internal displaced persons' camp. Food was scarce – particularly for a woman without a child. 'I wished to die,' Elizabeth said of her time in the camp. 'I lost all hope and life had no meaning to me.'

After three years in the camp, Elizabeth's village was finally safe for return. Yet her arrival saw old conflicts resurface as her in-laws tried to force her from her land. The local council rejected their claim and found in Elizabeth's favour, yet life remained bleak: 'I suffer from leprosy and I have lost some of my fingers to it. At that time I needed money for treatment, but I could not grow more crops because of the pain.'

I thought begging was the solution. I could not work to get whatever I needed so hopelessness and self-pity were my companions.'

Elizabeth's story may seem devoid of hope, yet after the pain of childlessness, after losing her husband, her security and her home, and after the struggle to rebuild a life in the face of such opposition, she finally encountered the local church. There she found hope – as well as faith and love in abundance.

Through attending a Tearfund-sponsored training, Elizabeth heard about the feeding of the 5,000 and felt her optimism begin to stir. She began cultivating more land, planting seven types of crop instead of her normal three and using the profits to buy a mattress, some clothes and a bull to help her plough: 'Things I had longed for but never hoped to have.'

'The church has become my family,' she says, referencing the volunteers who come and help harvest her crops. 'I live by faith in God and whether I have children or don't, God is my protection and I have put my faith in the Lord.'

This harvest you can get to know and introduce your community to the people of Ogongora and support them as you raise money. We're encouraging people to walk a mile in someone else's shoes to fundraise for people like Elizabeth. You could get your community involved, inviting your neighbours and local businesses to walk with you or sponsor you. Make the whole thing more fun by putting on your husband's, wife's, mother's, father's or neighbour's shoes, or try some silly clown shoes or maybe even go three-legged. You could get the children in your Sunday school or local schools to walk in their parents' shoes for a mile and see how much money they could raise.

Walk to school, to work or to church . . . wherever you want. Use the walk to get to know more people in your community; stop and chat to people on the way to tell them why you are walking. And when it's all over, why not gather everyone back after the walk for a harvest lunch or dinner?

For more ideas and for films and resources that will help you tell the story of Elizabeth's community, visit www.tearfund.org/harvest. Or if you are looking for a way your church can get to know and support a church overseas visit www.tearfund.org/connected. For other creative ideas to share your time and talents and connect your community with those living in poverty, visit www.tearfund.org/maketime.

Mission Organisations

There are many mission organisations that help provide for people living in poverty.
Find out how you can get involved by checking out their websites. Here are just a few:

Tearfund

Tearfund is a Christian international aid and development agency working globally
to end poverty and injustice, and to restore dignity and hope in some of the world's
poorest communities. They operate in more than fifty countries around the world.
As well as being present in disaster situations and aiding recovery through response
teams, they speak out on behalf of poor people on the national and international stage
by petitioning governments, campaigning for justice and raising the profile of key
poverty issues wherever they can.

For more information go to www.tearfund.org.

Compassion International

Compassion International exists as a Christian child advocacy ministry that releases
children from spiritual, economic, social and physical poverty and enables them to
become responsible, fulfilled Christian adults. They work through local churches
around the world and speak out for children living in poverty.

Find out more at www.compassion.com.

Methodist Relief and Development Fund (MRDF)

MRDF grew out of the desire to enable Methodist people to respond effectively, in the
context of global poverty and injustice, to the commandments of Jesus to love God
and love our neighbour. It aims to bring about significant and long term change in
some of the world's most marginalised communities, by supporting local development
projects and emergency relief, and empowering people to change structures that are
oppressive and unjust.

*They have free resources around harvest, which you can access via www.mrdf.org.uk/harvest
including worship resources and ideas for youth and children's groups.*

There are many mission
organisations that help
provide for people living
in poverty.

BMS World Mission

BMS World Mission is a Christian mission organisation, working in around 35 countries on four continents. BMS personnel are mainly involved in church planting, development, disaster relief, education, health, media and advocacy.

Harvest for Haiti

On 12 January 2010, it took 37 seconds for an earthquake to devastate the country of Haiti, home for little Pierre Ronald. Those 37 seconds killed more than 100,000 people, and made more than a million homeless, including Pierre. It was described as causing 'an almost unprecedented level of devastation'. The following weeks saw a global response, with rescue teams converging on the small island state, their every move filmed by the world's media. Actors, musicians and other celebrities gave their support to appeals for aid.

But now, a few years later, the world has moved on. Other disasters, including the Japan tsunami and the East Africa famine, have long since dislodged Haiti from the news. Today Haiti is still in turmoil. Little of the rubble from the earthquake has been cleared, thousands of bodies remain buried in the debris and visitors comment that the country looks like the earthquake has just happened. Children in Haiti are still dying from cholera and other entirely preventable diseases – children like Pierre. He contracted cholera from dirty water and very nearly died. He was saved only because he was taken to a hospital run by Christians, who treated him and loved him back to health.

This harvest, you can change a child's life with a gift of pennies.

For children like Pierre, a small tube of disinfectant and a pack of water purification tablets is the difference between life and death. Packs of these cost pennies, but are beyond the reach of the local people like Pierre's family. This harvest, you can change a child's life with a gift of pennies. Why not ask your church to raise funds to help us provide medical care, clean water and hope for Haitian children like Pierre?

To find out more about BMS's work in Haiti, visit their website www.bmsworldmission.org.

Caring for the Environment

Tearfund

What Does Climate Change Have to do With the Church?

Scripture reminds us that 'the earth is the LORD's, and everything in it' (Psalm 24:1). In fact, cast your mind back to the last beautiful sunset you saw or the last cliff-top walk you took and it's not only scripture that underlines God's ownership: the very earth itself speaks of God's love, care and creativity.

It's also clear that we haven't cared for the earth (and the people who depend on it) as well as we ought. We've gorged on resources that we should have protected, spewed carbon like it was going out of fashion and tried to ignore the issue while the death toll has risen.

> The earth is the LORD's, and everything in it.

As the impacts of our energy-hungry lifestyles take their toll and contribute to climate change, who picks up the tab? Take a look at the impact of the increasingly erratic and severe rain patterns, droughts and floods, and the evidence is obvious: these burdens land more heavily on the world's poorest people, who are already weighed down by poverty. They're the ones who depend on the land for food, the ones whose homes are built with too few resources and too many dangers. They're the ones for whom one failed harvest can lead to a poverty that is utterly overwhelming.

Yet the story does not end there. Hope is sprouting up around the world as churches and local communities respond to the change in climate. In Uganda, local churches are helping community members adapt by teaching new farming techniques. In Nepal, Christians are reaching out to neighbours affected by flooding. In the UK, thousands of Christians are giving generously, praying for mercy, calling on world leaders for justice and changing their lifestyles to better care for God's good earth and the people who live on it.

As well as local churches in poor communities rebuilding homes, planting trees and erecting flood defences – not to mention teaching new farming techniques that are better suited to unpredictable rainfall – there are also things that we in the UK can do to help.

If there is hope, then the church can offer it. We can play a key part in transforming the situation. We can change our own lives to live more in step with creation. We can convince our friends, our churches and our government that loving our neighbours involves sacrifice on our part. We can respond fully and without hesitation to what the psalmist says: that this world is created by and for God and that God's people depend on it.

Practical Ways to Make a Difference

Help your church and its members reduce their environmental impact, and show their thanks to God for creation in the process.

Work it out

Calculate your carbon footprint. Find out your individual, household and church emissions so you know where to concentrate your reductions. Check out Tearfund's My Global Impact – www.tearfund.org/mgi – to calculate individual emissions, or the Climate Justice Fund – www.climatejusticefund.org – for an example of average household emissions. Find ideas for churches to shrink their carbon footprint at www.shrinkingthefootprint.org.

Make the switch

Switch your home and church energy to a green energy supplier. This will cut your carbon emissions significantly and send a positive message to your community that you're taking action to tackle climate change. Tearfund partners with Ecotricity, who will donate £40 to Tearfund on behalf of every supporter who switches over through the scheme. See www.tearfund.org/ecotricity for details.

Go veggie

Encourage your church to have a meat-free Sunday. If everyone in the UK gave up meat once a week, the emissions savings would equal taking 5 million cars off the road.

Grow your own

Grow vegetables, herbs and fruit in your churchyard or garden. If you don't have one, use pots on a windowsill or in a sunny spot indoors. If someone in your church is a keen gardener, why not get them to put some information together for the local community about how they could grow their own veg and help the environment?

Phone recycling

Reuse and recycle mobile phones. Encourage your congregation to snub their next mobile phone upgrade and keep their current model instead. You can recycle any unused phones and donate the value to a charity.

Tech fast

Have a technology fast. Challenge your congregation to try a day with no TV, no iPod, no computer and even no mobile. Why not set aside a technology fast day each month?

Buy local

Reduce food miles. Buy seasonal and local fruit and vegetables, especially for your harvest supper event. To find out what's in season, visit www.lovebritishfood.co.uk. If you're buying goods from overseas, always go for the fair-trade option where possible.

Give away

Encourage your congregation to share unwanted possessions with people in your community through The Besom (www.besom.com) or Freecycle (www.freecycle.org).

Lobby

It's our job to speak up to remind the government to keep climate change high on their agenda.

We can all play a part in challenging injustice, pointing out to people in power that they have a responsibility to speak up for the poorest people whose voices are often ignored (Proverbs 31:8–9). Reducing our own emissions as individuals matters, but we also need action internationally to reduce global greenhouse gas emissions and provide money to help poor countries respond to the changing climate. Our government has the power to change the situation by working with other countries to agree international action. It's our job to speak up to remind them to keep climate change high on their agenda.

Encourage your congregation to write to your local MP to ask them what they're doing to tackle climate change and how they're urging the government to keep their climate promises.

Pray

Give thanks

God saw all that he had made and it was very good (Genesis 1:31).

- Give thanks for the amazing goodness of God's creation.
- Give thanks for the local churches around the world who sacrifice and serve to meet the needs of those whose poverty makes them vulnerable.
- Give thanks to God for bringing hope by equipping us to speak out to and pray for people in power.

Pray for change

- Pray that the church might also embrace real change.
- Pray that individuals and governments would do their best to reduce global emissions and provide money to the poorest and most vulnerable people who are hit hardest.

Pray for power

- Pray for God to move in power among those who make key decisions.
- Pray that truth and justice would be at the heart of political negotiations and that good decisions will be made that empower poor countries to respond to climate change.

EXTRA RESOURCES

BMS World Mission has a free DVD called *Future Shape* about creation care and the environment. With studies for individuals and groups, the DVD features leading Christian thinkers like Elaine Storkey, Sir John Houghton and Vinoth Ramachandra, www.futureshape.org.

Pray that truth and justice would be at the heart of political negotiations and that good decisions will be made that empower poor countries to respond to climate change.

HOPE OUTWORKED

Ways to Impact Your Community

Pray that your work will bear amazing fruit for God's kingdom.

The heart of HOPE is about you getting out into your community and sharing God's love in your words and actions. This section contains some great ideas that will help you maximise on harvest as a missional season, expressing your thankfulness in ways that will impact your urban or rural community. There are ideas that could be adapted for individuals, small groups, churches or groups of churches; some big, some small, but all of which seek to bless those outside of the church. They may help you meet new people you've not come into contact with, or build relationships with those you already know. You might find ways to freshen up a traditional event you hold, or perhaps use this as an opportunity to try something totally new. On page 121ff you'll also find some thoughts about how we communicate the good news of Jesus through our words as of course this is a vital part of our outreach. So get planning as early as you can to make the most of the opportunities around harvest, pray that your work will bear amazing fruit for God's kingdom and GO FOR IT!

> You could use your event as an opportunity to understand more about your community's needs! See page 75 for more details. It's also a great idea to have a box easily available with some small cards where people can post prayer requests.

Harvest Festival Services

Many churches hold a harvest festival, providing an opportunity to thank God for all that he has provided. This is a great chance to involve the wider community in your service, perhaps by inviting local businesses (see page 47 for more details) or how about holding your celebration outside of the church walls so it's easily accessible for all? You could:

- Hold an outdoor harvest festival at your local allotments and invite local schools to come along.
- Hold a celebration at a local supermarket.
- Build a bread oven as a church community project and invite local residents along for a bread- or pizza-making afternoon before or after the Harvest Sunday service.
- Consider calling it a Thanksgiving service in order to make it more accessible to members of the community.

How about using your harvest festival service as a chance to get people thinking about a lasting harvest? Ask people to consider what the harvest from their life will be, and to bring a symbol of this to the harvest service.

As part of your service, you may want to take up a food collection. Please see below for more ideas around this.

Idea for small groups

Hold a meal at your house, inviting friends from outside of church, and giving everyone an opportunity to say what they are thankful for.

Prayer idea for harvest festival

Encourage everyone to bring a picture of either someone or something for which they want to give God thanks or to bring a short prayer of thanks. Invite them during the service to come up and put their pictures or prayers on a prepared wall or boards, then have a time of thanksgiving in prayer, sharing scriptures and song.

Food Collections

For many, harvest is traditionally associated with collecting non-perishable food items and donating them to people in need in the community.

Make the most of your food collection by:

- Speaking to local charities to ensure your collection goes to those in need. You might want to support projects working with people who are homeless or living in women's refuge centres. Speak to the local council who will know about families that might be in need of a care package.

- Find out what your chosen charity would find most useful to receive and give suggested shopping lists to your congregation a few weeks ahead of harvest.
- Encourage your congregation to change their thinking from 'buy one get one free' to 'keep one give one away' in the run up to harvest.

Alternatives

- Instead of bringing food you could ask people to donate the money they would have spent and support a project either close to home or overseas. Make sure people are clear about where the money is going and how much of a difference it will make to the lives of those in need.
- Ask your congregation to donate pieces of fresh fruit, make them into small gift baskets, then give these out on the local streets as an act of kindness.
- Donate your time to local projects instead of giving money or food.

Food Banks

Great idea for a church or group of churches across an area

Food banks collect donated goods to provide a minimum of three days' emergency food for individuals or families in crisis. With 13 million people in the UK living below the poverty line, there are many around the country in need of help and food banks can be a straightforward way of helping those in need.

If there's a food bank in your area consider supporting it, either by providing goods for their harvest collections (many food banks will have a list of helpful items to donate at harvest) or by sending volunteers to help sort the boxes and deliver them. If no food bank already exists, you could speak to the Trussell Trust about how you could set one up for your area, www.trusselltrust.org/foodbank-projects.

We asked one church in London about their experience running a food bank and here's what they told us:

Hillingdon Food Bank

Hillingdon Food Bank launched in 2009 and was the first food bank in London. It provides a breathing space, supporting individuals and families through the tough times by providing short-term and emergency food supplies to families going through difficult times in the borough, through a referral system from frontline professionals in the council, GP surgeries, social services, NHS and Job Centres.

How does it work?

Food is collected by volunteers from supermarkets, individuals, churches, school harvest festivals and other organisations. It is sorted in the warehouse and banked ready for distribution to those in need. The food bank works in partnership with voluntary and statutory agencies which come into contact with people in crisis through the course of their work.

Partners issue vouchers which the clients bring to the food bank centre and exchange for a week's worth of food. Three days is the period assessed as the minimum time it takes for agencies to be in a position to offer assistance. Realistically, we know that it may take longer so we will extend our support where appropriate.

As the client waits for their food to be packed, they will be offered a cup of tea or coffee and the opportunity to talk to a worker about their situation. Where appropriate, the worker may signpost the client to agencies that can provide specialist support and assistance.

Results

Hillingdon Food Bank has supported over eight hundred people in need in the Hillingdon borough with food packs and supported the setting up of other food banks in the London area. The Hillingdon Food Bank was the Mayoral Charity of the Year 2010/2011 in the borough. The Hillingdon Food Bank was also nominated for Hillingdon Local Heroes Award 2011 and was issued a certificate for Highly Commendable Community Champion to appreciate the good work it has done. Food Bank Services have received positive feedback from partners and clients who have benefitted from their services.

Examples of those helped locally are:

- A project manager whose team member committed suicide; he got sacked and had nothing.
- A 60-year-old British national who emigrated to live in the US for 40 years and was deported with nothing after his partner died. The food bank helped with food and clothes.
- A returnee soldier from Afghanistan, hungry for 48 hours and separated from his family.
- A family who lost their home in a fire and needed emergency food.
- A family who lost their business due to the economic situation.
- Several people going through relationship and family problems.
- Individuals going through an adjustment period due to bereavement.
- Several people waiting for, or turned down for, crisis loans and about to go hungry.
- Several professionals made redundant and trying to get new jobs.
- Several single mums who were choosing between paying bills and feeding their children.
- Families with children struggling on one income or low incomes.
- People deep in debt and almost giving up were supported with a food supply.

> **Turn some local wasteland into a garden** which not only looks good but where food can be grown to give to local people in need. You could run simple teaching sessions alongside this on how to grow your own vegetables.

Harvest Suppers

Ideas for individuals, small groups and churches

Harvest is a brilliant time to bring your community together for a celebration. There are countless different ways you could make your harvest supper special as you welcome in members of the community. Here are some things to consider:

Food

You could have a food tasting festival.

- You could grow the food yourselves, suggesting a menu and things for your congregation to plant ahead of the event.
- Why not eat a typical meal from the developing world but charge the typical price of a Western meal and donate the money to charity?
- Hold a 'bring and share' meal so the responsibility is split between everyone who comes.
- You could have a food tasting festival, inviting people to bring unusual or exotic dishes.

Costs

You may want to make the meal totally free as a blessing to your community or you could ask for donations and then split them between charities (e.g. a local Christian charity, a local project run outside of the church and an overseas project).

Venue

You could use your church, hire the village hall or make it an intimate event in your home and invite your neighbours. If the weather is warm enough, you could have a picnic or a party in the local park.

Entertainment

- Play games or run a quiz.
- Have a live band.
- Hold a ceilidh or barn dance.

As an alternative you may want to hold a café-style event with coffee, cakes, quizzes and games.

Community Survey of Thankfulness

Go door-to-door in your neighbourhood and ask residents what they are thankful for and what they most need.

• Use the data to inform future outreach projects.

• Use the opportunity to invite the people you speak to along to church.

• Use the data as part of your harvest service, giving an overview of what people in the area are thankful for and praying for their needs.

• You could use a response card if you don't have time to go door-to-door yourself.

• Ask people if they have any prayer requests that you can intercede for during harvest. You may want to leave them a postcard to fill in and drop back to you.

Or how about visiting local shops, businesses and schools in your community and asking individuals what they are thankful for in your area? Take photos of them and then create a display in your church of the photos and sound bites as a way of celebrating the harvest of the local area. You could also leave the people you speak to with an invitation to come and see the display and attend a harvest service.

Random Acts of Kindness

Why not take the opportunity to bless your friends, family and neighbours with an act of kindness?

• Leaf raking for neighbours.

• A week before the clocks change, drop cards round to local houses reminding them to change their clocks. You could also attach a small gift or offer to pray for them and their needs.

• Make cookies and cakes and hand them out in a public space. Also give out a bookmark giving thanks to God for all he gives us at harvest time and details of church services/Alpha courses running in the town.

• As a church take a market stall and donate the money raised from produce sold to a local charity.

• Publish a free sheet and distribute locally with good-quality articles that members of the congregation are willing to give away free.

• Open up your church for an afternoon so people can come and see the harvest flower displays and share a cream tea.

• Offer to wash people's cars free of charge.

Prayer and Food!

Each day we eat foods from all around the world. Why not take up the challenge to count how many different foods from different places you eat in a day? Perhaps as a small group you could share your findings and pray for the places the food came from. Give thanks to God for all the people represented in the chain bringing that food to your plate. You could share the idea with colleagues and friends, or do the project with children.

You could hold a special night of prayer for drought-torn areas around the world and for UK farmers or find out more about where food is produced in the UK using www. goodfoodnetwork.com. You could use a map to trace where all your food comes from and use it as a prompt for prayer.

Ideas for Kids

Harvest musicals and sketches

There's a whole range of harvest musicals containing catchy songs and readings, aimed at different age groups from Key Stage 1 through to older teenagers. They are available from www.redheadmusic.co.uk and are ideal for schools.

Or you could put on one of the musicals with your Sunday school and take it out into the community – perhaps in a shopping centre, a hospital, a retirement community, a local park or even a service station. Hand out song sheets so that everyone can join in, and perhaps give away something to eat or drink. You could have collection buckets to raise money for charity at the same time.

HOPE has a brand new harvest sketch and accompanying drama workshop material for you to download for free! Written by Anna Turner and Saltmine, *Scarecrow's Stormy Day* is a 5- to 10-minute sketch that can be performed by primary-school-aged children in harvest services and assemblies. Set against the agricultural background that we associate with harvest, it focuses on themes of generosity, friendship and thankfulness. Download it for free at www.hopetogether.org.uk.

Further ideas

- Go on a nature walk and collect as many seeds as you can (conkers, acorns, berries, grasses, etc.). Help the children identify them and talk about sowing seeds and harvesting.
- Write prayers for those in need on fruit and vegetable cut-outs.
- Support a charity that works overseas but also learn about how the charity helps people, where it works and the food and farming methods of the country.

- Put on a drama such as the one below discussing the importance of saying thank you:

Zac does not like getting up on a Saturday morning (. . . who does?). Mum calls him several times to come and get his breakfast. When he appears he refuses to say grace.

'Why should I say thank you to God for my toast? God didn't make my toast; Mum did.' Then [very begrudgingly] 'Thank you, Mum, for my toast.'

Mum refuses to accept the credit saying, 'All I did was to put the bread into the toaster. It's no good thanking me; you should thank the people at the Co-Op [or any other outlet] for the bread.'

So Zac goes to the Co-Op and says thank you to the baker who works in the bread department, who says, 'It's no good thanking me; you need to thank the delivery man who brings the ingredients to make the bread' . . . who says, 'It's no good thanking me; you need to thank the miller who makes the flour' . . . who says, 'It's no good thanking me; you need to thank the farmer.'

Now the farmer goes to Zac's church. When Zac appears and makes his little speech, the farmer takes Zac to a field and tells him that all he does is sow the seed. God sends the sunshine and the rain, the day and the night, and God makes the seed grow. So, really, he needs to say thank you to God . . . at which point you can explain that harvest is saying thank you to God for all that he provides.

Creative ideas

- Squashing berries and using the juice to dye pre-cut banners to be hung in the church. (Make sure you know which berries to avoid!)
- Making bread.
- Flower arranging.
- Collages with autumn leaves, etc.

Community Prayer Treasure Hunt

A 60-minute adventure outside of your church building praying for your local community.

- Begin inside the church building. Prepare your hearts and minds before you start.
- Put people into small teams of different ages. Give each team a colour.

- Explain that there are clues hidden in plastic boxes around your local community. Colour coded envelopes, one for each team, are inside these boxes. No stealing or tampering with other team envelopes!
- Explain that each team will be on a different route around the game, so their first clue will take each team to different starting prayer boxes.

Select from the following Prayer Box ideas to design your own prayer time or make up your own! Five or six boxes will probably be enough for a 60-minute time frame. Teams will need time to walk between prayer stations. Choose carefully the geographical area to be used. Walk and time it ahead of the event!

Box 1: Faith like mustard seeds

Jesus told us all we needed was faith the size of mustard seeds.

Put this box outside a school or key building of influence. Inside, place mustard seeds in small bags, one for each team participating. Put an instruction sheet that says: 'Take the packet of seed for your team and divide it equally among yourselves. Jesus told us all we needed was faith the size of mustard seeds to remove obstacles to the kingdom! Examine the seed. Now each one of you spend 5 minutes sowing your prayers of faith for the school [or other place] where you are. Plant the seed or throw it to the wind. What will you dare to pray?'

Box 2: Jesus, the Bread of Life

Place this box in a park or on a piece of grass. Put in enough slices of bread for each team. Either scatter bread in your local park for the birds or eat it yourself! Spend 5 minutes praying that there would be a growing hunger for truth in your community and to know the purpose of life. Ask God for opportunities to share this bread – and hope – with others.

Box 3: The Lord's Prayer!

Make a photocopy of the famous model for praying that Jesus gave his disciples. Each person must choose a phrase or a line from it. Turn this line or phrase into a prayer as you walk to the next box. Teach the younger ones how to do this. For example, 'Our Father' – 'Thank you for being our Father, for being the Dad who loves the people in the home I am walking past. Bless them, Father . . .'

Box 4: Prayer shapes!

In this box write the instruction: 'Your task as a team is to make the word HOPE with your bodies!' (Take a photo on your mobile to prove it later to the other teams!) Read out loud the scripture from Romans 15:13, 'May the God of hope fill you with all joy and peace as you trust in him, so that you may overflow with hope by the power of the Holy Spirit.' You could say this scripture a few times and make it a prayer for your community, changing the word 'you' for the name of your town, village or city.

Box 5: Egg-timer blessing

Place this box close to another church in the town or community. Write a note that says: 'Use the egg-timer! Turn it over to start the prayers. Pray all together as one, for as long as the timer lasts. Pray heaps of blessings upon that other church (leaders, youth, families, children, etc.) and see if you can last the time!'

Box 6: In the bag!

In this box place two or three pairs of rubber gloves and one black bin liner per team. Place this box in a street where there will be some minor rubbish to pick up. Instruction note: 'For 5 minutes use the gloves and bin liner to pick up bits of rubbish from the street. As some of the team do this everyone is to ask the Lord to send the Holy Spirit to convict the community of the rubbish in our lives and to make people aware of the consequences of their sin and God's wonderful gift of repentance and new life in Jesus!'

Idea provided by Andy Kennedy of King's Kids, YWAM England.

Harvest Labyrinth

A labyrinth combines the imagery of the circle and spiral into a winding path, inviting anyone to slowly walk along the path, with different stopping points allowing personal reflection, interaction and prayer about their spiritual journey and their relationship with God, their community, our planet, etc. This could be laid out in a church or church hall, or put up alongside any community activity, e.g. a harvest supper. It can be done just for those within the church family or it can be modified to be used by anyone in the community.

> A labyrinth combines the imagery of the circle and spiral into a winding path.

You could do your labyrinth based on the journey of a grain of wheat to a loaf of bread, having stopping points which include a tray of soil, seeds to plant, watering and shining light on the soil, a growing plant, harvesting the wheat, grinding the wheat into flour, and a loaf of bread. At each point provide something to interact with, something to reflect on, something to do and something to pray. Use biblical texts to draw out implications with the seed to our spiritual journeys and where we are all at.

For more details please visit the HOPE website www.hopetogether.org.uk.

Rural Mission Ideas

In addition to the ideas on the previous pages, these may be particularly useful for celebrating harvest in rural churches.

Celebrate British Food!

Harvest is a brilliant opportunity to support and celebrate British produce!

Harvest is a brilliant opportunity to support and celebrate British produce! British Food Fortnight is traditionally held in September/October (in 2012 it takes place earlier in the year because of the Olympics) so it's ideal to link to your harvest celebrations. The aim is to make the public – and in particular young people – aware of the diverse and delicious food that Britain produces and to increase awareness of the health benefits and pleasures of eating quality, fresh, seasonal and regional produce.

Also a great idea for urban churches!

- Link with others in your community who would be interested in celebrating local food, e.g. local shops, schools, pubs, farms, markets, restaurants, hotels and schools.

- Explore how raw materials are turned into the finished product – show the process and provide tasting opportunities for the finished products.

- Arrange a harvest supper on a farm with local food and drink, a short act of worship in a barn, and finish with a barn dance.

- Ensure that any church catering, particularly during this season, uses local food and drink and fair-trade products.

- Contact local organisations that have a meal as part of their life, e.g. schools, Rotary, lunch clubs, old people's homes, and suggest they organise a special meal that celebrates British food. Offer someone from the church as a speaker.

- Hold a seminar on the importance of harvest and local business and farming.

- If others are holding a harvest event, talk to them about using British food, and perhaps offer a small additional worship element, like an opening prayer or an easy-to-sing hymn.

Hold a Harvest Festival Weekend

Make a splash with your harvest celebrations by making a whole weekend of them.
Put on a free family event where you could include:

- A children's farm.
- Children's harvest-themed craft activities.
- Face painting.
- Horse-drawn wagon rides.
- Live music.
- A special harvest lunch on the Sunday, using fresh seasonal local produce.
- A celebration service on the Sunday.

For more information on how this was done at Winchester Cathedral, see http://winchester-cathedral.org.uk/2011/09/14/a-hampshire-harvest.

With thanks to Gordon Gatward, OBE, for providing many of these ideas.

Make a splash
with your harvest
celebrations by
making a whole
weekend of them.

Your Harvest Stories and Ideas

Local food festival

One church held a British sausage festival ahead of their harvest festival with everyone's favourite type of sausage provided by local producers and butchers. They served mash made from British potatoes with local cream, salads and home-produced puddings. Then during their harvest festival the sermon was about being proud of our farmers and afterwards they had another feast of wonderful British home-cooked ham, beef, jacket potatoes and salads followed by homemade apple pies (British apples of course!).

Farm walk and sheep roast

In addition to their usual services, another church held a farm walk and sheep roast. Members of a suburban church from Northampton joined in and together they visited a farm and learnt something of what life is like for those in agriculture today. The sheep roast was washed down with excellent Northamptonshire wine. The event was a great success in building links between suburbs and country as well as between consumers and agriculture.

Organic harvest festival

The rector of five parishes in Devon arranged for a harvest festival at Riverford Organics (which produces organic food boxes). It included a tour of the Riverford site, followed by a short service and lunch in the restaurant.

Following the food chain

Laurencekirk, in the heart of rich farming country in the north-east of Scotland, has seen the decline in agriculture break the connection between people and the land. The church ran a local food event on a Saturday reflecting each part of the food chain in the area, with a simple soup and roll lunch provided by the congregation. 'Harvest of the Mearns' included fruit and vegetable growers, a grain merchant, whisky distillery, beef producer, preserve manufacturer and bakery supplier. Over 300 people visited the event and the attendance at harvest festival the following day doubled.

Harvest auction

Sheep feature prominently throughout life in the North Yorkshire Dales, particularly in the rural market town of Hawes, in Wensleydale, during September when the annual two-day sale of Gimmer lambs is held. An annual evening harvest service is held on the Sunday following the lamb sales where harvest produce is auctioned off for money to be given to small local chapels. A harvest banner is draped around the auctioneer's stand, from where the preacher leads the service; sawdust is scuffed around the floor as Hawes Prize Silver Band arrange seats in the ring, ready to accompany the singing. The congregation takes their place where farmers and buyers recently stood. They reflect on the work of the charity Shelterbox in the context of the auction ring and step away from the comfort of their church buildings, seeking to learn more about communities less fortunate than themselves.

Service for lambs or snow!

Some communities in Scotland, such as the Angus Glens and parts of Highland Scotland, see harvest as being in the spring and so hold a 'Service for the Lambs'. Others have marked their thankfulness for snow where this has brought out the skiers; harvest need not just be in the autumn!

Charitable harvest

The Methodist Church in Hawes decided some years ago to devote half of its annual Harvest Sunday morning collection to some other charity, aside from local church funds. Since 1998 an additional service has been held in the local Auction Mart, with a nominated charity (Christian Aid, Water Aid or Farm Africa) benefitting from the collection. As the years have passed, this service has drawn in the other local churches and is now arranged by Churches Together in the Hawes area, and is usually accompanied by the Hawes Prize Silver Band.

> The service was held in the grain store of a local farm.

A farm service

The service was held in the grain store of a local farm with worship taking place in front of a pile of recently harvested beans, with tractors parked outside. It was led by one of the local team of clergy and included an interview with the farmer who was questioned about the harvest, the crop in the store, etc. This then became the focus for the congregational prayers.

The young people's group organised a quiz during the service on the theme of 'bread', linking it to Jesus' declaration of himself as the 'bread of life'. The guest preacher was from the Arthur Rank Centre and the sermon focused on farming and food production.

The members of the congregation were invited to stay on after the service for refreshments. The harvest loaf was taken from its prominent position in front of the congregation and cut, buttered and shared with everyone, along with either a glass of wine or fruit juice.

Although the service wasn't Eucharistic there was a strong Eucharistic feel to what was experienced as the climax of the service. The atmosphere was informal and relaxed and those present who weren't regular attenders at worship felt welcomed and at ease.

Rural activities for children and young people

- Ask what was eaten for breakfast or bring a shopping basket full of foods, e.g. apple, pear, malt cereal, porridge, bread, baked beans, dried beans, potatoes, crisps, fresh and tinned carrots, coffee, sugar, tea, etc. How do these products arrive at our dining table? Older children could draw flowcharts of the production process.

- Interview a farmer or someone involved in the food chain.

- Ask if anyone has seen farmers working in the fields. What processes did they see? What machines were the farmers using?

- Discuss what wheat makes and discuss the different stages of making bread (planting, cutting, harvesting, milling, baking and eating). Use a bread maker to bake a loaf during the service/assembly/session.

- Focus on one local food and tell its story, tasting it if possible. Find some recipes for traditional harvest fare or local delicacies, e.g. Shropshire Fidget, Damson and Apple Tansy, Suffolk Fourses Cake, and bring some to eat.

- Explore some local harvest customs, e.g. making corn dollies.

- Explore the benefits of eating seasonal food. What food is in season at the moment?

- Explore what fair trade might mean for local farmers.

- Ask a local primary school to take on a charity per class that they can give needed produce to. They could make special boxes and write messages to go with the gifts.

- Grow wheat and arrange a visit to a local mill for it to be milled. You can thresh and winnow the wheat as a class activity, and after the visit you can make bread with the flour, perhaps even using a clay oven in the garden, www.sustainweb.org/realbread/bake_your_lawn/.

Ask a local primary school to take on a charity per class that they can give needed produce to. They could make special boxes and write messages to go with the gifts.

Remembrance Day
The 11th of the 11th

Laurence Singlehurst

Remembrance Day and Remembrance Sunday fall into the harvest period so it's worth us considering some activity focused around this memorial. Churches have historically been very good at Remembrance Sunday, with most respecting a two-minute silence within their Sunday service. However, increasingly, local communities are taking note of the 11th of the 11th as well which often falls midweek and tends to focus around the village, town or city war memorial site. In my town at ten minutes to eleven there is very little happening around this site but over the last few years, as it creeps up to eleven o'clock, suddenly several hundred people appear as if out of nowhere and stand respectfully in silence as the last post is sounded.

Let's think of ways we can stand with our community as we remember those who have fought in past wars and those who continue to risk their lives in current conflicts. The sad reality is that many members of our churches and communities are still touched by the worry and pain of having loved ones in the forces. Let's stand with them and show our respect for their sacrifices.

> We remember those who have fought in past wars.

We asked churches around the country how they honour Remembrance Day and these were the ideas they gave us:

- Participate in the civic remembrance parade, service and wreath laying.
- Alternatively hold your own parade, joining with local groups and armed services representatives to take a walk of remembrance. You may need to talk to the police about shutting roads on the route to traffic. Lead the parade towards your church and hold a service of remembrance there, before holding a two-minute silence at the local war memorial.
- Take Armistice Day services in local schools.
- Have a live link to the remembrance service at the London Cenotaph beamed onto a screen for five minutes during church morning worship.
- Hold a special service to remember people who have died during the last twelve months in your community.
- Give opportunity in your service for people to speak about their own experiences in the armed forces.
- Remember those who have 'fallen' by reading their names and lighting a candle for each of them within the church service.

- Hold a remembrance service in the local primary school, using researched information on the children's ancestors.
- Use the breaking of bread and sharing of wine in remembrance, as Jesus taught us. This could be extended to having a community meal where there is an opportunity for the community to talk about their own experiences or share memories of service men and women.
- Give financial support to relevant charities who care for wounded service men and women and care for the bereaved.
- Hold a service in the police canteen on Armistice Day.
- Explore what it means to be peacemakers today with testimony or stories of people working for peace throughout the world.

RESOURCES

- British Legion: www.britishlegion.org.uk
- National War Museum: www.cwgc.org/education/rememberme.htm
- www.ctbi.org.uk/resources and the book *Beyond Our Tears: Resources for Times of Remembrance*, (CTBI, 2004), £7.95.

Use the breaking of bread and sharing of wine in remembrance, as Jesus taught us. This could be extended to having a community meal where there is an opportunity for the community to talk about their own experiences or share memories of service men and women.

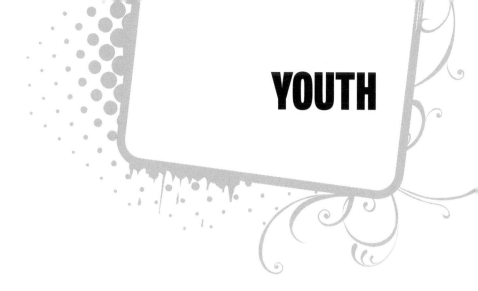

YOUTH

Mission Ideas for Young People

The HOPE Revolution is all about seeing young people get out of their comfort zones for Jesus and expressing his love through what they say and do. We want to see young people take risks for Jesus, becoming 'Change Agents' in their communities and living the radical adventure that is being a disciple of Jesus Christ. Here are some harvest mission ideas particularly suitable for young people.

Invading the Streets During Harvest

Here are a number of ideas to see young people take an expression of God's love and our thankfulness to the streets and to the heart of our communities.

'Give Us This Day Our Daily Bread'

A great idea to meet a practical physical need over a lunchtime period.

What's the idea?

The earth is satisfied by the fruit of his work . . . wine that gladdens the heart of man, oil to make his face shine, and bread that sustains his heart (Psalm 104:13,15).

Create an opportunity for a group of young people to take to the streets one lunchtime where they set up a stall to make sandwiches to be given away. This can act as a reminder of God's provision and goodness to us, that he does indeed provide our daily bread. The stall could display scriptures such as Psalm 104:13,15, and young people can use this as an opportunity to express God's love that is made free to all.

Things to consider

Offer to pray a blessing upon people.

- Prepare clear signage for good visibility.
- Hygiene: ensure antibacterial hand wash is used and visible as well as catering gloves and aprons worn by all.
- Utilise cool boxes to keep fillings fresh.
- Provide ample table space for sandwich preparation.
- Pre-prepare all sandwich fillings, grated cheese, ham slices, egg mayonnaise, sliced cucumber, sliced tomato, diced lettuce, with salad cream and dressings available. Provide sandwich bags and napkins.
- Provide information on harvest services or church activities, such as Alpha, for customers.
- A number of young people could be available for conversation whilst others are preparing sandwiches.

Thankfulness Expressions

An opportunity to encourage the community to reflect on the things for which they are thankful, and to remind them that all good things come from God.

Praise the Lord

Who satisfies your desires with good things so that your youth is renewed like the eagle's (Psalm 103:5).

What's the idea?

Get your young people together for an afternoon, where they take to the streets with a 'thankfulness' sign and flip-charts. Young people can ask passers-by to write on the flip-chart something for which they are most thankful, allowing participants to consider being thankful to God.

Things to consider

- Having publicity to hand out for youth clubs and church events.
- Giving out flyers which provoke thought about God's goodness to us.
- Offer to pray a blessing upon people, that they may know more of God's goodness and the fullness of life.

- Find creative ways of displaying suggestions. Perhaps have the word 'thankfulness' written in large letters, with participants suggestions being written on Post-it notes and stuck on to the letters.
- Give out sweets as a 'thank you' for participating.
- Have Gospels available for those who engage at a deeper level.

Harvest 'Fruits of the Spirit' Stall

The fruit of the Spirit is love, joy, peace, patience, kindness, goodness, faithfulness, gentleness and self-control (Galatians 5:22).

Challenge your young people to offer prayer to passers-by who recognise their need for differing fruits of the Spirit.

What's the idea?

Set up a harvest 'Fruits of the Spirit' stall with nine different sections of fruit labelled love, joy, peace, patience, kindness, goodness, gentleness, faithfulness and self-control. Ask passers-by if they would like a free piece of fruit, and to choose one which represents something they would like more of in their life at this time. Offer them the chance to receive prayer to know and receive more of their particular chosen fruit of the Spirit, and let them know that this is something that God gives to us.

Things to consider

- Perhaps a local supermarket or grocer would be prepared to discount or even supply you with some free fruit.
- Present your stall well, with the fruits clearly shown and labelled.
- Young people to act like market stall traders, calling out 'Amazing fruit that can last for ever! Come and get some life-changing fruit here!'
- Use sweets such as Rosy Apples and Sherbet Lemons instead of fruit to save space and money.
- Pray blessing over the passers-by.
- Give fruit to people who are homeless and ask if they would like to talk about the fruits of the Spirit.
- Invite people to a Youth Alpha course where the Holy Spirit is explained in more detail.

£5 Giveaway

An opportunity for young people to be creative in ways to bless others.

What's the idea?

Get your young people into groups of two or three and challenge them to bless members of their community by spending £5 in the most creative and beneficial ways. Use this as an opportunity to direct any thankfulness for the actions to God.

Things to consider

Love the Lord your God with all your heart.

- Seeking God's guidance and leading on who and how to bless.
- Buying cards to thank people in the community for the things they do.
- Giving away Love Hearts sweets to let people know they are loved.
- Buying £1 umbrellas for those who may be getting wet.
- Buying a meal for a homeless person.
- You will need to complete a full risk assessment and put in place clear boundaries for the young people.
- Approach the church to financially back this event, putting aside the necessary money.
- Get the young people to do a fundraising event to raise the money to be given away.

Invading the Community During Harvest

Love the Lord your God with all your heart and with all your soul and with all your mind . . . Love your neighbour as yourself (Matthew 22:37–39).

An opportunity for young people to be challenged to love and serve their local communities through what they say and what they do.

Harvest 'Mowing and Reaping'

An occasion for young people to do a random act of kindness for the residents of their local community.

What's the idea?

For young people to offer a free lawn-mowing service, emphasising our call to care for God's creation and using it as an opportunity to bless their local community.

Things to consider

- How could the people most in need of help be targeted?
- Wearing T-shirts profiling the initiative for maximum visibility in the community.
- Using this time to pray for the occupiers of the house, and to inform them about church activities.

Risk assessments should be completed to ensure all necessary safety precautions are taken, e.g. using circuit breakers, safety training for using lawn mowers, activity to be completed in small groups with adequate level of supervision.

Further ideas

How about also offering: fence painting, raking up leaves, garden clearing and general garden maintenance?

Harvest Sports Competition

An opportunity to celebrate our health and give thanks for our bodies, involving young people in community sports challenges and competitions.

What's the idea?

Hold a half-day harvest sports event, giving young people the opportunity to engage in a variety of sports and competitions. Use this as an opportunity to build relationships and bless the youth of the community, whilst empowering your youth to lead and facilitate these activities.

Things to consider

- In addition to a football, hockey or rounders competition, consider having some specific 'harvest-themed' challenges that could utilise food, e.g. food eating challenges or relays involving a variety of foods.
- Conclude the activity with a barbecue (for a small fee).
- Give away trophies, medals, prizes and/or certificates.
- Utilise sports that can draw in all ages and both genders.
- Have a prayer team praying for the young people who participate.
- Develop a regular sports activity for the community.

Other community activities could involve litter picking, graffiti clearing, fence painting, and could serve local community centres, schools, residential homes as well as individuals and families in the community.

Invading Your School During Harvest

Why not use harvest as an opportunity to thank our schools and teachers for all they do to support young people? Additionally, how about expressing thankfulness for God's creation and all of the earth's provision in our schools and use it as an opportunity to bless those less fortunate than ourselves?

School Food Hampers

What's the idea?

Challenge your young people to an initiative inviting pupils in their schools to provide hampers of non-perishable foods for the vulnerable in the community.

Things to consider

Think about how you can get teachers and the school on board.

- Think about how you can get teachers and the school on board with this initiative.

- Perhaps a letter could go out to all students following an assembly devoted to harvest.

- Get your Christian Union to deliver the assembly, or involve local youth leaders in the project.

- How about consulting with the local authority to identify suitable projects to support, such as a women's refuge centre, a local project for homeless people, a local project reaching out to the elderly, etc.

24-hour Fast

A 24-hour fast could be a great way to raise money for a local, national or international project that helps feed people who are in need.

- Participants could fast for just one meal if they weren't able to do the full fast, or could fast from another activity for a longer period (e.g. not buying chocolate or fast-food for a week and donating the saved money).

- If you ran the fast through a school, consider putting on an activity over the lunch period such as a prayer time for people who are starving in parts of the world.

- As alternatives to a full fast, young people could:
  - eat half portions of their meals and donate the money saved
  - exchange their dinner money for a piece of fruit or a protein bar
  - be encouraged to donate their change from their lunch.

Permission to fast from food should be gained from parents. For some it is inadvisable to abstain from food on medical grounds.

Bless Your Teacher

Use harvest as an opportunity to thank your teachers for their investment in you, to show your respect and appreciation for all that they do.

- Buy them some chocolate or flowers.
- Write them a card of personal thanks.
- Get the whole class to present a gift, flowers or card, explaining that harvest is a time of thanksgiving.
- Ask if there is a task that your class could do to help them.
- Leave an anonymous gift on their desk.
- Get your homework in on time!

Use harvest as an opportunity to thank your teachers for their investment in you, to show your respect and appreciation for all that they do.

Youth Group Sessions

Urban Saints

Session 1:
Lord of the Harvest

The aim of this session is to try and make young people aware of all the good things that God gives us, and also to be aware of those who are not as fortunate as us. Through this it is hoped that they will learn not to take food for granted and be empowered to pray for and help those who do not have as much as we do.

Share

Isn't it funny when someone says a word to you which makes you think of a song that you simply can't get out of your head? For me it was the word 'harvest' and the lines:

Lord of the harvest, Lord of the field,
Give thanks now to God, in nature revealed.

Author unknown

We remember how God created seeds that grow into plants. The first two lines of this hymn remind us that harvest is all about God and the ways that he provides for us. This is why we give thanks at harvest time, as we remember how God created seeds that grow into plants, which provide food to satisfy our hunger. God is the Father of creation; the Father of harvest and that is why we celebrate harvest once a year. This is a very biblical thing to do. Exodus 23:14–19 tells God's people the three annual festivals that they should be celebrating, of which harvest is one. We are told to bring the best that we have to honour and praise God for his goodness to us (v.19). Some churches still ensure that harvest is a big occasion. I have memories of harvest festival services from my childhood when I attended a Church of England school. There used to be a huge display of food at the front of the church, with every fruit and vegetable imaginable! At the centre was a large loaf of bread, which had been made in the shape of wheat. However, the challenge today is to try and retain this festival and make it relevant in today's culture and society.

Today we are distanced from how our food is grown and where it comes from. Very few of us grow our own vegetables, and supermarkets stock fruit and vegetables all year, when in fact some of their seasons only last a few months. Modern technology has enabled us to enjoy our favourite fruits all the time by importing them from other countries. We live in a culture of supply and demand. However, with that comes the tendency to take it all for granted. We can forget those in the world who do not have enough food and for whom life is a struggle of trying to keep their families and themselves alive. People are malnourished and ill because they do not have food and clean water. Harvest is a time to give thanks to God for all he provides us with but it is also a time when we should remember all those in the world who go hungry. As we praise God for all we have, we need to pray for and remember those who have nothing and seek God's guidance as to how we can help them.

We need to pray for and remember those who have nothing.

Getting Started

GAME: DUNKING FOR COLOURED APPLES

The point: a food game linked to harvest.

Duration: 15 mins

Equipment required: one apple per person, towels, food dye, bowl/kitchen sink and water.

Description:

- Fill the sink/bowl with cold water and a few drops of food dye.
- Put the apples into the water and get the group to take it in turns to take the apples out of the water using their teeth. They could put their hands behind their backs to stop them from using them!
- Have towels ready for when they come out of the water – the food dye simply adds an additional mischievous twist to the game (it is a good idea for the group members to put a towel over their clothes to protect them from the dyed water).

Or

QUIZ: WHAT AM I?

The point: a fun introduction to the theme.

Duration: 10 mins

Equipment required: (make beforehand) a piece of card with a selection of different seeds stuck onto it, e.g. sunflower seed, a pumpkin seed, an apple pip. Label each with a letter. You will also need pens, paper and a prize for the winners.

Description:

- Split the young people into small groups or pairs depending on the size of the group and how many quiz cards you have managed to make.
- Give the groups a quiz card with the seeds on, some pens and paper.
- Give the groups five minutes to name as many of the seeds as they can by putting the letter name and then their answer onto the paper. You might like to provide a list of possible answers for them to try and match up.
- When the five minutes are up, go over their answers. The winners are of course the ones who have got the most correct seed names.
- Discuss with the group that sometimes seeds can look really similar, e.g. a sunflower seed and a butternut squash seed. Sometimes they can be really different, e.g. an apple pip and a sunflower seed. It is very hard to guess from looking at a seed what it will grow into with a bit of care.
- Talk to the group about how wonderfully and beautifully made the world is. Discuss with them how amazing it is that a small seed can grow into a piece of fruit or a vegetable that can keep us alive.
- Encourage the group to remember how the food we eat started out – that a juicy, red apple began life as a small, brown and hard pip.

Or

COMPETITION: READY . . . STEADY . . . TASTE!

The point: to introduce harvest by getting the group to think about and taste the good things that we have.

Duration: 15 mins

Equipment required: a selection of fruit and vegetables (e.g. mango, melon, apple, carrot, passion fruit, sharon fruit, kiwi fruit, courgette, cucumber, etc.), 2 blindfolds, 2 plates, several spoons, a couple of cloths to cover the plates, a table, 2 chairs, and pen and paper to keep score.

Please be aware of any food allergies that members of your group may have.

Description:

- Prior to beginning this activity, cut up a selection of fruit and vegetables into small bite-sized chunks – make sure that you still know what they are! Put them onto the two plates and cover them up to keep them fresh.
- Put the plates out on a table with a chair at either end of the table and a blindfold next to it.
- Split the group into two teams and get the teams to choose their first taster, who should come and sit on one of the chairs and be blindfolded.

- Select a piece of fruit or vegetable for both of the tasters and put it into their mouths using a spoon.
- Ask the taster to guess what fruit or vegetable they just ate. If they get a correct answer, mark it down on a piece of paper.
- Swap tasters to ensure that several people get a go.
- The winning team is the one with the most correct answers.
- Talk to the group about the many different varieties of fruit and vegetables that we have to eat, how they all taste and look different and are grown in a variety of ways. Explain to them that harvest is a time to give thanks to God for the wonderful variety of food he has blessed us with.

Digging In

BIBLE STUDY: THE MIGHTY SEED

The point: to help young people to realise in a simple and visual way that the seeds that God created become food for us to eat and how amazing that is!

Duration: 20 mins

Equipment required: Bibles, pictures of seeds, pictures of trees, packet of mustard seeds or cress seeds, kitchen roll, cotton wool and enough yoghurt pots for every member of the group.

Description:

- Show the group some of the seed images and ask them to remember these images as you read Matthew 13:31–32 together:

  He [Jesus] told them another parable: 'The kingdom of heaven is like a mustard seed, which a man took and planted in his field. Though it is the smallest of all your seeds, yet when it grows, it is the largest of garden plants and becomes a tree, so that the birds of the air come and perch in its branches.'

- Discuss with the group how amazing it is that a tiny seed will grow into a tree that will have deep roots to hold it straight and strong, a firm trunk that will support all the leaves and branches, and that even though seeds are so small, they can grow into bigger and better things.

- Show the group pictures of trees and put them alongside the ones of the seeds.

Read Luke 21:29–31:

  He [Jesus] told them this parable: 'Look at the fig-tree and all the trees. When they sprout leaves, you can see for yourselves and know that summer is near. Even so, when you see these things happening, you know that the kingdom of God is near.'

When you see these things happening, you know that the kingdom of God is near.

- Discuss with the group that when we see trees with their leaves in bloom, we should remember God's kingdom and creation. It should remind us that the trees started off as a tiny seed that grew into something amazing just as God planned.
- Tell the group that in order to visually appreciate how amazing this all is, that they are going to witness the mighty seed in action! Explain that they are going to grow some mustard or cress seeds and, although they will not grow as big as trees, they will grow big enough to eat.
- Give each member of the group a yoghurt pot, some kitchen towel, some damp cotton wool and some mustard or cress seeds.
- Get them to put the kitchen roll into the bottom of the yoghurt pot and then put the damp cotton wool on top. Next, sprinkle some of the seeds and place the pot in a sunny place. Within a few days the seeds will germinate and in a week they will have grown and the young people will be able to harvest their crop and eat it!

Or

BIBLE STUDY: I NEED A VOLUNTEER PLEASE

The point: to get the young people to think about what they can do to serve God and to empower them to do it.

Duration: 20 mins

Equipment required: Bibles

Description:

Read Matthew 9:35–38:

> Jesus went through all the towns and villages, teaching in their synagogues, preaching the good news of the kingdom and healing every disease and sickness. When he saw the crowds, he had compassion on them, because they were harassed and helpless, like sheep without a shepherd. Then he said to his disciples, 'The harvest is plentiful but the workers are few. Ask the Lord of the harvest, therefore, to send out workers into his harvest field.'

Jesus had a way of talking that made people think.

As a group discuss:

- What is Jesus telling the disciples to do?
- Why does he use the festival of harvest as an example of what he is talking about?

Jesus is telling the disciples of all the work that needs to be done amongst mankind. He likens this to gathering in crops at harvest. When the crops are gathered in from the field, the farmer needs a lot of helpers to do it. Jesus is comparing humans to being the crop. He needs more people to go out and share about what he did for humankind on the cross and what it means to them. The trouble is that people are not always willing to go and do this for him. He needs more workers.

Read Matthew 28:16–20:

> Then the eleven disciples went to Galilee, to the mountain where Jesus had told them to go. When they saw him, they worshipped him; but some doubted. Then Jesus came to them and said, 'All authority in heaven and on earth has been given to me. Therefore go and make disciples of all nations, baptising them in the name of the Father and of the Son and of the Holy Spirit, and teaching them to obey everything I have commanded you. And surely I am with you always, to the very end of the age.'

This passage is entitled 'The Great Commission' for it is at this point that Jesus clearly states what he wants his disciples to do. Jesus tells them to go out and tell the world about him and how much he loves them. Jesus calls his disciples to go into the world and serve him and to help others to believe and serve him also. Harvest is all about the gifts that God has given us, the food that sustains us. It's about thanking God for this and remembering what he does for us. This passage is about a different sort of harvest. It is about how people who believe in Jesus need to go and tell others about his love so that they may believe too.

Ask the group to spend some time reflecting on their own quietly, or split into smaller groups. Ask them to think about two things:

- First, ways in which other people have tried to tell and show them about Jesus. Which of these have been good, positive encounters and which have not been so great?
- Second, ways that they might feel they could tell others or show others of Jesus' love and salvation.

Harvest is all about the gifts that God has given us, the food that sustains us.

Response

PRAYER: LORD OF THE HARVEST

The point: to encourage young people to thank God for all that they have and to remember and pray for those who have little or nothing.

Duration: 10 mins

Equipment required: pictures of people affected by drought, by floods and people harvesting their fields.

Description: Pass the images among the group as you read out the prayer:

People affected by drought:

Lord of the harvest
We thank you for the sun that helps our plants to grow. We pray for all the
people who suffer because there is too much
sun and their crops are ruined, which leads to them and their families
being hungry.

People affected by floods:

Lord of the harvest
We thank you for the rain that stops our plants from dying of thirst. We pray,
Lord, for all those who suffer because too much rain has flooded their homes and
their crops.

People harvesting their fields:

Lord of the harvest
We thank you that we can plant seeds and watch them grow into plants that
we can harvest as food to sustain us. We pray for the people whose crops have
been damaged or destroyed, with the result that that there is no food for them to
harvest. We ask, Lord, that you will help us not to take food for granted and to
remember those who have so little.

Amen.

We thank you for the rain that stops
our plants from dying of thirst.
We pray, Lord, for all those who
suffer because too much rain has
flooded their homes and their crops.

Session 2:
Thankfulness and Generosity
Small group session
Share

A student group at De Montfort University decided to live on rice and beans for seven days and to give the money they saved on food to a local charity supporting homeless people. Why? They wanted to understand what it feels like to live off less every day, to put themselves in someone else's shoes and 'love their neighbour as themselves' (Matthew 22:39). The Bible gives an inspirational invitation to followers of Jesus to feed the hungry, clothe the naked and provide shelter for the homeless. This group of students wanted to step up to this invitation and see life through someone else's eyes, stirring up conversations with friends about how fortunate we are to eat what we want, when we want. They also wanted to raise money to help find resources and food to support the homeless in Leicester.

How did they find it?

'All I want is some flavour in my life! As a lover of food I'm finding this very difficult but at the same time totally amazing that I depend on food so much! It is really making me appreciate how lucky we are and it's crazy that some people have to live on this their whole lives. Only three more days to go until we go back to normality, although I think it will affect me and I will continue to talk about it for the rest of my life.'
Coral

Reflect

As we hit pause on our busy lives and reflect on what we do have, rather than what we don't, we realise that we live in one of the richest nations in the world.

Watch Miniature Earth (www.miniature-earth.com) and reflect on the fact that if you keep your food in a refrigerator, your clothes in a wardrobe, if you have a bed to sleep in and a roof over your head, you are richer than 75 per cent of the world's population.

> Reflect on what we do have, rather than what we don't.

Act

Read Matthew 22:34–40:

> Hearing that Jesus had silenced the Sadducees, the Pharisees got together. One of them, an expert in the law, tested him with this question: 'Teacher, which is the greatest commandment in the Law?'

Jesus replied: "'Love the Lord your God with all your heart and with all your soul and with all your mind.' This is the first and greatest commandment. And the second is like it: 'Love your neighbour as yourself.' All the Law and the Prophets hang on these two commandments.'

When is the last time you gave something up in order that you might have a greater appreciation of it and better understand someone else's situation?

Cultivate an attitude of gratitude.

Why not consider the following ideas:

• Live on rice and beans for a weekend or a whole week.

• Don't buy any new clothes for six months.

• Fast from TV for a week.

• On your next birthday ask people to donate money to your favourite charity rather than giving you presents.

• Live on 10 litres of water a day for one week. (Tearfund's *Turn it Up* resource will equip you to take on this water challenge. You can download it at http://youth.tearfund.org/campaigning/Turn+it+up/.)

Be intentional about telling people what you're doing and why. Update your Facebook status and/or tweet about how you're finding it. Choose to be someone who, by what you say and do, speaks on behalf of the last, the least and the lost.

Commit

Cultivate an attitude of gratitude. Write a list of all the things that you're grateful for and encourage the group to take their list away, and to look at it each morning as a prompt to thank God.

A grateful heart is a generous one. As we become more thankful for what we do have, generosity is a natural outflow of the heart. Discuss what you could do as a group to be more generous with (1) your money (2) your words (3) your time.

Pray

Close your session with a time of giving thanks to God.

For more small group material from Urban Saints please visit http://energize.uk.net/.

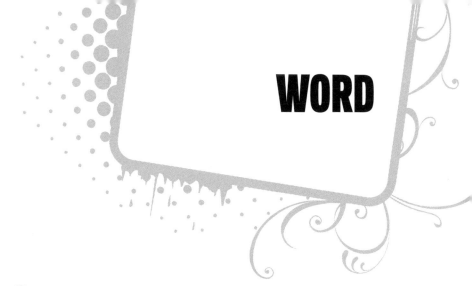

Communicating the Gospel with Our Words

Roy Crowne

To communicate the gospel we need to use both our words and our actions. Many of the ideas within this resource relate to the actions so here we want to focus on the importance of the word element. If we want people to know about God, at some point we need to communicate what we believe, and tell them about Jesus and what he has done. It often seems that this is the place where we have the most difficulty. The great thing about focusing on harvest, generosity and thanksgiving, is it provides us with an amazing opportunity or 'hook' on which to build our message.

The first key is to know your audience.

Here are some keys you may find helpful as we journey together to seek to effectively communicate the message of the gospel in these environments, whether it is at our harvest festival, harvest supper, Thanksgiving dinner or service, or any mission activity.

The first key is to know your audience. In other words think about the context of the event and the people who will be there. This was something that Jesus was brilliant at doing. Whether it was talking about the leaven in the bread, farming or money, his stories and parables were about things that people knew and understood. He then moved from there to the truths that he wanted to present. Let's present the gospel with the language, signs and symbols that people can relate to.

The second principle to be effective in communicating the gospel is to tell people what they know to be true. The parable of the sower talks about various different soils where the seed of the word of God is planted in each soil but has a different impact. Telling people what they know to be true opens them up to an 'Aha!' moment where they realise that what is being said is reality in their lives. The Bible says that truth is written on people's hearts, so when we tell them what they know to be true we are building credibility and believability.

Pray that Jesus would be seen through our words and actions.

The final piece of advice is that Jesus would then put the message into a kingdom context. He didn't seem to feel that he had to tell the whole gospel, but could leave that one seed that the Holy Spirit could use to bring people along on their journey of faith. We don't have to cram everything in to each event, but perhaps reflect on one aspect of the gospel that seems to fit the context, and pray that Jesus would be seen through our words and actions and that he would draw people to himself.

The Bible says that truth is written on people's hearts, so when we tell them what they know to be true we are building credibility and believability.

Extending an Invitation

Michael Harvey

Many of us cannot remember the last time we invited someone to church, because we have simply stopped inviting people. One reason might be that we fear someone saying 'no' to our invitation, or perhaps we've asked people before and been disappointed by their response. Why do we give up so easily? I have heard countless stories from Christians who had to be asked several times before they ever accepted an invitation to attend church for the first time. We need to learn from the persistence shown in the stories of the Lost Coin and the Lost Sheep, where a true persistence and determination was shown because the thing that was lost was worth searching for. It would also help us to remember that 'success' is doing our bit and inviting someone; we cannot control or claim responsibility for the answer they give. It's OK for someone to say no, the important thing is that they were invited.

Some of us fear that we might spoil a good friendship. We don't ask because we fear it will cause irreparable damage, but frankly it is very unlikely that we are going to spoil a true relationship over a simple invitation. And of course there's every chance it might change the relationship for the better! But fear of being rejected can just stop the whole process. I have been rejected hundreds of times and yet I still often take it personally. I have to remind myself that it's not a rejection of me; that person is just not yet ready to come to church. We need to be people who live by faith rather than fear. Fear stands for false (F) evidence (E) appearing (A) real (R). Fear is a thief that steals and destroys but it will only become big if we allow it to grow. We can stop it growing by recognising it; then we can resist and reject it. Our doubts and fears will usually step aside when we make an unyielding commitment to action.

> We need to be people who live by faith rather than fear.

For church members to feel confident in extending invitations, it's also important for church leaders to be clear about seeker-friendly services. Harvest is a great time to have a guest service and for church leaders to tell their members in advance how that service will be delivered so they can feel confident in asking friends. A service themed around thankfulness will be appropriate for all, giving an opportunity for members of the community to come and give thanks for their families, homes and food.

So let's all take courage this harvest and be generous in inviting others to come along to our church activities and services, for by doing so we will reap a rich harvest.

Michael Harvey is the co-ordinator of Back to Church Sunday.

Back to Church Sunday

Back to Church Sunday is an opportunity to extend an invitation to friends or family and ensure they receive a warm welcome when they come to church. To make the most of Back to Church Sunday, hold it the week before your harvest celebrations and make sure you invite people who attend to join you for your harvest service the following week.

You can find out more about Back to Church Sunday and order resources at www.backtochurch.co.uk.

RESOURCES

Unlocking the Growth, Michael Harvey (Monarch, 2012), £8.99

A book about the power of invitation; looking at how churches can grow through the congregation inviting their friends.

The Big Welcome

It is about making people feel really welcome in any church activity. The Big Welcome is a simple campaign to encourage Christians simply to invite someone they know to something they love. With its roots in Back to Church Sunday, this initiative, a partnership between Elim, the Methodist Church, the Baptist Union of Great Britain and the Baptist Union of Wales, is about making people feel really welcome in any church activity.

The word 'church' is purposely not in the title so you can be really creative about what you would invite people to, whether that's a meal, a concert, a quiz night, a coffee bar or even a church service.

With the theme around 'God's Big Embrace' and the story of the Prodigal Son, the Big Welcome is an initiative by which churches can encourage people to take an invitation, trust in the power of prayer and take big steps in reaching out to their friends and family. The Big Welcome is supported by resources including posters, invitation cards, prayer cards and a bookmark giveaway, alongside service resources, teaching resources and resources for churches in their planning, to get ready to truly make church, or an event, a really welcoming occasion, without the cringe. (The invitations and posters are available in both English and Welsh.)

For more information and to access resources visit www.thebigwelcome.org.

Releasing the Workers for Evangelism

Mark Greene

As a church leader, you naturally want your congregation to be engaged in mission and evangelism all the time. The reality, however, is that they can't be engaged in mission and evangelism *in the same way* all the time. Every context is different – work, neighbourhood, door-to-door, mums and toddlers, Alpha – so your people all need to be supported in prayer but they need to be equipped in different ways.

As it relates to workplace evangelism, the three dominant emotions that a huge number of Christians feel are guilt, fear and inadequacy. They feel guilty because they think that evangelistic conversations are the only thing that really counts to their church – and they just don't get that many opportunities. They feel fearful because they rightly recognise that the people they share the gospel with today are going to be the people they share the office or the building site with tomorrow and it might go horribly wrong. They feel inadequate because maybe they haven't seen much fruit and don't seem very good at taking the opportunities that do come their way.

Well, with that in mind, there's a great opportunity for church leaders who want to help. Sometimes, however, church leaders feel ill-equipped to know precisely how. The most important thing, however, is not that you have the perfect evangelism model for every possible context but rather that you are a leader who wants to encourage your people for a life of workplace evangelism that is purposeful but not driven, Spirit-sensitive not impatient, bold but not impetuous, loving not mechanistic. And that you, like them, are ready to learn and use your own wisdom and skills and resources to help them work out the ways forward.

Your people all need to be supported in prayer but they need to be equipped in different ways.

There are lots of practical ideas for your people in my book *Thank God it's Monday* but here are five things you, as a leader, can do:

1. You can reassure and envision

You can remind your people that God loves their co-workers.

And because he loves them he is quite likely to be actively working in their lives to draw them to himself. The Christian may be the only Christian in the workplace, and very significant for that reason, but they may not be the only person or means of communication that God is using in the non-Christian's life: there's the witness of the word, the witness of creation, the witness of other Christians, the witness of the Spirit and the witness of miraculous divine intervention.

Secondly, you can remind Christians that they spend quite a lot of time with the people they work with. So there's time to build credibility and trust and relationship. That said, you can also reassure them that you understand that, though there may be lots of opportunities to show the gospel in a day, there are usually rather fewer opportunities to share it.

> **Remind workers that God is the evangelist. He draws people to himself.**

Thirdly, you can remind workers that God is the evangelist. He draws people to himself.

As his people we do what we can in loving, cheerful obedience to his call and in the power of the Holy Spirit. And then we leave the results to him. Sometimes people see fruit instantly, sometimes it takes years, sometimes we find out in heaven.

2. You can demonstrate that you want to understand

Every workplace is like a foreign country. And they can be as different from one another as Norway is from the Sudan. It's one thing, for example, to be a young waiter in a suburban restaurant where the other waiters and waitresses are all young, the atmosphere open and there are plenty of opportunities to chat about life, the universe and Jesus. However, it is quite another thing to be a young lawyer in a city law firm working seventy hours a week, where every minute has to be accounted for, everyone around you is a rival and people don't tend to go much deeper in personal conversation than the latest episode of *EastEnders* or the football results. The point is that usually the opportunity to share a testimony or the gospel arises out of a relationship where the person trusts the Christian enough to let them in. And that will take a whole lot longer in that city law firm than in that restaurant.

So, you can ask your people questions, find out what their particular work is like, what the people are like, what someone's boss is like. You could simply decide to use five minutes after every service to ask one person a week: 'How do you see God working in your daily occupation?' After a while that will change your congregation. One of the most transformative things pastors can do, according to those who have done it, is to visit someone in their workplace. You might aim for one person every six weeks. You may never visit everyone but the word will get round that you are interested and that will send a powerful message to your people that God is too. Beyond that it will almost certainly further enrich your preaching, teaching and prayer.

3. You can pray and you can enlist pray-ers

Prayer is the most powerful tool we have. So you could begin to pray systematically for your workers – annotating a church list with information on where they work and what they do. You could look at the church's prayer diary and make sure that work is included with other missional areas.

You could encourage home group/cells/life groups/pastorates to pray for each other's non-Christian co-workers by name. It only has to be one person and people who don't work outside the home can bring the name of someone they are concerned about.

4. You can harvest stories of fruitfulness and blessing in the workplace

Testimony inspires. And as people begin to hear stories of fruitfulness they too will recognise how they may already be fruitful themselves and how God might use them. Ideally, these need to be shared publicly – either in a service or through a newsletter.

5. You can ask workers: What would help you be more fruitful?

Some people will need some training to be ready for and alert to opportunities, others might need help in identifying a next step. Pathways abound: from a Christmas card, to a Christian book on an issue, to a novel with an interesting theme that triggers a conversation, to a verse for a particular occasion, to a one-on-one Bible study in the local coffee shop before or after work, to an invitation to a talk in a curry house/course in a home/service in a church . . . to a barbecue, to a Cup Final party, to a bake-in for the homeless in the Christian's home . . .

Just imagine what God might do through your church's ministry among the people they spend so much time with at work.

The Lord be with you. And them.

Testimony inspires. And as people begin to hear stories of fruitfulness they too will recognise how they may already be fruitful themselves and how God might use them.

Acknowledgements

Roy Crowne
Executive Director: HOPE

Board

Steve Clifford
Evangelical Alliance

Andy Hawthorne
The Message Trust

Mike Pilavachi
Soul Survivor

Steve Price
HOPE Together

Leadership Team

Yemi Adedeji
Jesus House

Wendy Beech-Ward
Spring Harvest

Matt Bird
Make It Happen

Ian Bunce
*Baptist Union
of Great Britain*

Gavin Calver
Youth for Christ

Rob Cotton
Bible Society

Joanne Cox
Methodist Church

Jane Holloway
World Prayer Centre

Ann Holt, OBE
Bible Society

Dr Rachel Jordan
Church of England

Bishop Wayne Malcolm
Christian Life City Church

Ade Omooba
*Christian Concern/Christian
Legal Centre*

Kiera Phyo
Tearfund

Laurence Singlehurst
Cell UK

David Westlake
Tearfund

Thank you to everyone who
has contributed ideas, articles
and help to this resource
including:
Simi Adedeji, Tunde Balogun,
Paul Bayes, Craig Borlase,
Hanna Bullock, Ian Chisnall,
Lucy Cooper, Ken Costa,
Revd Joanne Cox, Paul
Farrington, Revd Dr Gordon
Gatward OBE, Thandi
Haruperi, Michael Harvey,
Pastor Agu Irukwu,
Abbot Christopher Jamison,
Graham Jones, Dr Rachel
Jordan, Andy Kennedy,
Beth Milburn, Chris Smith,
Helen Taylor, Victoria
Thompson, Phil Timson,
Dan Wilton and Debbie
Wright.

Special thanks to Mark
Greene for providing the
workplace materials, to
Stewardship for providing
the small group materials, to
Urban Saints for providing the
youth group materials, and to
the team at Authentic.

Written and compiled by
Liza Hoeksma
Edited by Liza Hoeksma and
Laurence Singlehurst
Project co-ordinated by
Steve Gee

Designed by Mike Thorpe at
The Design Chapel

Contact HOPE at:
8A Market Place
Rugby
Warwickshire
CV21 3DU

Tel: 01788 542782
Email: info@hopetogether.org.uk